THE

ADMINISTRATION OF IOWA

A STUDY IN CENTRALIZATION

BY

HAROLD MARTIN BOWMAN

AMS PRESS
NEW YORK

COLUMBIA UNIVERSITY
STUDIES IN THE
SOCIAL SCIENCES

46

This Series was formerly known as
Studies in History, Economics and Public Law.

Reprinted with the permission of Columbia University Press
From the edition of 1903, New York
First AMS EDITION published 1969
Manufactured in the United States of America

Library of Congress Catalogue Card Number: 70-82248

AMS PRESS, INC.
NEW YORK, N. Y. 10003

TABLE OF CONTENTS.

CHAPTER I.

THE ADMINISTRATION OF IOWA: ITS BASIS AND PROBLEMS.

CHAPTER II.

PUBLIC EDUCATION.

98567

CHAPTER III.

CHARITIES AND CORRECTIONS.

PAGE

CHAPTER IV.

PUBLIC HEALTH AND SAFETY.

CHAPTER V.

PUBLIC FINANCE: INCOME AND ADMINISTRATION.

CHAPTER VI.

CONCLUSION.

SPECIAL ABBREVIATIONS.

L. = Laws; L. S. B. E. = Laws of the State Board of Education.
D. C. C. = Debates of the Constitutional Convention of 1857.
C. J. = Council Journal; H. J. = House Journal; S. J. = Senate Journal.
S. F. = Senate Files; H. F. = House Files.
S. R. = Reports of the State Superintendent of Public Instruction.

CHAPTER I

THE ADMINISTRATION OF IOWA: ITS BASIS AND PROBLEMS

THE problem of administration in Iowa is the universal problem of the American State of to-day, that of the proper apportionment of powers between the State and the local government. Responsibility, efficiency and freedom in administration, this is the triple end sought in the efforts toward improvement of government, an end upon the attainment of which many of the unrealized ideals of democratic society depend.

There is little in the institutions of Iowa to distinguish it markedly from other States. In the years preceding 1850 it had the characteristics common to pioneer government, many that two hundred years before had stamped the seaboard colonies. Penalties for refusal to serve in local offices, meetings of the townsfolk to regulate their local affairs, *viva voce* voting not only upon minor matters, but upon the acceptance or rejection of their early Constitutions; through this familiar stage the community, with the laws and traditions that it had inherited, was almost bound to pass. Now and then it devised governmental machinery of its own, such as that embodied in the firm covenant of the Land Claims Associations, but usually its political and social inheritance was found adequate to its needs.

The broad outline of the government of to-day is substantially that of the second year of its independent territorial existence. The territorial government as first organized was modeled upon the Northwest Ordinance of 1787, by which the Governor had a wide appointing and the absolute veto powers.   But the great friction between the Governor and the Legislature, which led to a petition on the part of the Legislature to the United States Congress for a change, early resulted in the limitation of the executive power.   However, from the beginning to the present time the Governor has almost always been a prominent and often, through his moral influence, almost a controlling force in the State.   Legislatures have often consulted his wishes, and been influenced by them as much as by his veto power or his administrative authority.   Such direct administrative power as he has possessed has been confined to the central State interests.   Local officers and local interests have, except in the most rare instances, depended in no manner directly upon his will, as they have at times in Eastern States.   As a member of the Executive Council and of various State boards and commissions, he has exerted a strong advisory influence, while at the same time he has participated in their administrative functions.   He has authority to appoint commissions to examine the books and accounts of State officers.   If any defalcation, misappropriation of funds or improper and unsafe keeping of books is found the Governor has power to suspend the delinquent, and it would seem that in many cases the suspension might be equivalent to a removal.   This power, though possessed since 1858,[1] has seldom or never been exercised.   At the same time he has had a rather limited power of appointment which he has exercised alone, with a branch of the General Assembly or some State board or officer.

By his side is a central executive body of extensive powers, the Executive Council.   Created in 1851 under the name of the Census Board, primarily for the control of the

[1] *L.*, 1858, c. 160; *Code*, 1873, § 759; *Code*, 1897, § 1259.

State census, and composed of the heads of the several more
important departments, and indeed including the Governor
himself, from time to time it has been given powers which
have made it a factor in almost every branch of the State's
administration.   Direct administrative power or wide supervisory authority have in many cases been bestowed upon it.
And it has been the recipient of many miscellaneous duties
which the Legislature, as though at a loss for a more con-
venient factotum, has often referred to it.   Among its more
important powers are those of assessment of certain corporations and general equalization.   Certain other duties
are the change of towns to cities of the second class, and of
cities of the second class to those of the first, the approval
of bank depository bonds, the making of appropriations from
the providential funds, powers with reference to building
and loan associations, the canvassing of State election returns, and certain appointive powers.

The sphere and the organs of city government have been
little altered from their early character because of the
growing population or changing services.   There have been
complaints at times of local shortcomings, but they were
seldom long sustained, and the instances in which there has
been any very significant change from the early system, in
which rule of the city was by a council, with the Mayor
little more than the presiding officer, have been very infrequent.   Such changes as have been made have tended
toward the increase of the Mayor's power.   In 1902 a Civil
Service Commission was provided for the city of Des
Moines, the members of which were to take office under the
Mayor's appointment.   And in various other directions his
powers have been extended.   Formerly city marshals were
elected by the people.[1]   They are now appointed by the

---

[1] *Revised Statutes*, 1860, §§ 1103, 1106.

Mayor, as are policemen and police matrons, and the Council may provide other offices shall be filled in this way. Appointive officers in cities and towns hold office subject to dismissal for cause by the appointing power.

That greater change has not taken place in municipal government, and that it has been, if not brilliant, seldom corrupt and often satisfactory, is to be attributed largely to laws of the fortunate character possessed by certain provisions of the Constitution of 1857. While in many instances early city charters had imposed a limit upon the borrowing powers of the city, in some this power was entirely unlimited, the only condition being the consent of a certain per cent. of the electors. However, in 1857, when the new Constitution was adopted, the indebtedness of municipal corporations was limited to five per cent. on the value of the taxable property within their limits.[1] The occasion for this limitation was chiefly the large debts that had been contracted by local divisions in the aid of railways.[2] This movement did not get under way in the other States until twenty years later.[3] In this Constitution also Iowa took an early step in prohibiting the incorporation of cities and towns by special laws,[4] though this has been to a degree evaded by the familiar device of municipal classification and general legislation for the single class, which class has sometimes in effect comprised but a single city.

These few facts perhaps suggest what may be described as the chief characteristic in the development of the Iowa administration—that of an even progress, a gradual growth

---

[1] *Cons.*, 1857, art. 11, § 2.   [2] See *Gov. Mess.*, 1856, pp. 13, 14.

[3] Henry Wade Rogers, *Municipal Corporations*, in *Two Centuries Growth of American Law*, p. 242.

[4] *Cons.*, 1857, art. 3, § 30. The statement in Rogers, *op. cit.*, p. 247, that Iowa led the way in this matter is erroneous. The Constitution of 1846 not only did not prohibit such incorporation; it expressly sanctioned it. See Art. 8, § 2.

or accumulation of strength and fitness, rather than a sudden enlargement. This, though a somewhat subjective factor, must be borne in mind if the meaning of the changes in the administration and their results are to be comprehended. There have been a few deviations, some—for instance the county judge administration of 1851 and the State Board of Education of 1857—as novel experiments in government as have been made anywhere in the United States, but as a rule the even course has been undisturbed. Politics, industry and social relations have been characterized by the same poise and natural development. There have been striking exceptions here as well; occasionally a factious struggle has become virulent and disgraceful, but as a generalization the truth of the statement will hold. Iowa has grown symmetrically and in all directions. Nowhere is this better illustrated than in the growth of the population. In this the rural districts and the towns both have participated. It is true that the population of the cities shows a tendency to increase more rapidly than that of the rural districts, but the very fact that there is an increase in the rural population, while in some States of the same general character as Iowa, notably Ohio, Indiana, Illinois, Nebraska and Kansas, there has been an actual decrease, is indicative of conservative tendencies.[1] Moreover, the semi-urban population has increased much more rapidly than the urban,[2] a fact that well illustrates the pursuit of a middle course. Iowa has no large cities. The railroads have often been blamed for this. It has been pointed out that from 1870 to 1890 the net increase in population in Illinois, Wisconsin, Iowa and Minnesota, except in the new section, was in towns and cities that were given competitive rates, while

[1] *Twelfth Census of the United States*, vol. 1, p. lxxxix.

[2] *Ibid.*, p. xc. In the decade, 1890–1900, of the total increase in the State the rural population counted 14.6, the urban 38.3, and the semi-urban, 47.1 per cent.

all those having non-competitive rates decreased in population.[1]   The lack of large commercial or manufacturing
centres is ascribed to this, and as a further consequence
there has arisen the necessity of crossing the State line to
market a large part of the produce.[2]   But whatever the
force of this argument, the State has been, and will continue
to be, primarily agricultural, and the manufacturing me-
tropolis is not likely to arise within its borders   The
importance of this fact in an administrative connection will
hardly be overestimated.   At once those difficulties which
have arisen in States having large cities, difficulties that
have often led to a separate and distinct administrative
policy for such cities, are eliminated.   The State administration becomes a unit; what is applicable in one part is
applicable in another.   In New York, Ohio and Illinois the
larger cities have strained the balance of government.   In
Massachusetts their individuality has given rise to differentiation.   In Iowa these things have not been known, and a
symmetrical administration has been possible.

But the essential problem of administration is as near to,
and perhaps as far from, solution in Iowa as elsewhere.
That problem, as we have said, is one of responsibility, efficiency and independence in the administration, both State and
local.   To solve it there is necessary, on the one hand, the
careful delimitation of the sphere of the State; on the other,
that of the local administration.   It will be asked in what
way can that sphere within which the city or town or township should be allowed to rule itself be made distinct, so
that it may be known when and when not the State en-
croaches upon its powers?   And how shall the State's domain of authority be so clearly defined that the local division

[1] A. B. Stickney, *The Railroad Problem*, p. 62.
[2] F. H. Dixon, *State Railroad Control*, p. 204.

when acting as the State's agent and servant shall have no
excuse for perversion of that agency or any pretence that it
is acting on its own behalf?   The question should be
answered in a practical way, a way that will recommend
itself to the natural processes of legislation.   And that
can in part be done.   Allow the State to attract to itself,
and itself administer those powers which as near as can be
told appertain to it as the State.   Permit then the city or
local division to exercise untrammeled the authority that,
so far as it shall appear, belongs to it as the local government.   Relieve it of the tutelage of the interfering Legislature.   The results will at first be rough.   But when the
true line of cleavage has been established the finer adjustments can be made with little difficulty.

It is with the first part of this process that this essay has
to deal—the degree to which the administration of the
State's powers has been attracted to the State's hands.   This
is the primary task, and a work upon which the State has
already entered and accomplished much.   And as the State
thus becomes stronger in its own authority, gradually there
may be brought home to it a knowledge of the effects and
injustice of its interference in affairs purely local.   For the
foundation of local home rule already exists; the Legislature
has been ordered to withdraw where it has made too great
inroads.[1]   The functions of the State and the functions of
the municipality have their distinctive places in the theory
of the law, but much is to be done before they shall be
brought into efficient and just relations.

In thus defining the scope of this essay it becomes obvious
that neither State government nor local government *per se*

[1] *State vs. Barker*, 89 N. W., 204.   It is remarkable that this case, decided in
February, 1902, was the first in which the position of the city and its relation to the
State was defined.   Of course, many preceding cases had hinted at the relation.
See *State vs. Des Moines*, 103 Ia., 76.

is to be discussed. The subject matter is to be found in the intermediate ground, that ground where both the State and the local government exercise powers of administration, and, primarily, where the local government acts as the agent of the State. It is here that the more complex problems of administration are to be found, and it is this ground that must be cleared before the full definition of State and local authority can be made. Those functions which are indubitably State or local, and which are exercised accordingly, will not be touched, except incidentally, though in them there are many problems of surpassing interest. For example, the questions of State expenditure, or State budgetary practice, or the construction and powers of the Executive Council, or, on the other hand, in municipal government, the question of the relations of the Mayor, the Council and local boards and officers; these subjects all invite analysis and criticism, but they are not directly within the scope of State centralization. The subjects that will be treated of are public education, charities, corrections and penal institutions, the public health and safety, and public finance in so far as it concerns State income and income administration.

CHAPTER II

PUBLIC EDUCATION

I HISTORICAL SKETCH OF THE ADMINISTRATION OF THE SCHOOLS

THE history of the school administration of Iowa has been one of development in both the local and the central divisions. The chief powers of school government are, and have ever been, in the hands of the local school officers, in the Boards of Trustees and directors. It is not, however, to be denied that the central authority has exercised a wide influence, and that that influence has been exercised through channels of efficient control. For though the local bodies have been shorn of little of their powers, though indeed new powers have been given them from time to time, there yet have been significant accessions of authority to the State administration. When new functions have suggested themselves to legislators the tendency has often been to confer the attendant power upon the State rather than the local instrument.

In examining historically the development of the school administration in Iowa we have no such key to the State control as is found in those States that have made school support a branch of the State finance. The support of the schools in general has been left to the townships, towns, cities and counties. The school fund is not a gratuity of the State, though the State acts in the distribution of that fund. It is rather a gift of the National Government, for it comes from the public lands, and is expressly conditioned

upon devotion to the use of public instruction, a use to which
the State has pledged its honor repeatedly in Constitutions
and statutes.   Moreover, the revenue from the school fund
defrays but a small part of the school expenses.[1]   In one
field, that of higher education, the State has raised and
spent its bounty, and here it has exercised substantial authority.   Because of the absence of State aid, then, we
should not be surprised if the centralization were very weak
indeed.   That such is not the case, that there is a fair degree
of central control, must therefore be imputed to other forces.

The relation of the central authority to the schools begins
soon after the creation of the territorial government.   Laws
were on the statute books of Michigan and Wisconsin when
Iowa was organized as a part of those territories providing
for public instruction, but the Michigan government was
absentee, that of Wisconsin hardly immediate, though for
a season Burlington was its territorial capital; and this,
together with the fact that there was practically no school
population at this early date, makes consideration of these
laws needless.   In fact, until about 1854 there was relatively
little material and little need for schools.[2]

[1]Year.	Expenditures.	Annual Interest of Permanent Fund.	Year.	Expenditures.	Annual Interest of Permanent Fund.
1849	44,738	6,138	1880	4,921,249	282,903
1854	121,965	50,155	1885	6,054,313	248,260
1860	655,938	142,151	1890	6,710.317	266,338
1865	1,265,667	138,840	1895	8,317,875	235,663
1870	3,043,420	238,356	1900	9,028,918	118,700
1875	4,605,749	318,997	1901	9,321,652	108,942

[2] *Cf.* Jesse Macy, *Institutional Beginnings in a Western State,* in *Johns
Hopkins Univ. Studies in Hist. and Pol. Science,* vol. ii, pp. 365, 366.   It
would be erroneous to assume that all the schools were private and none public in
the early history of the State.   The report of the territorial superintendent in 1841
is sufficient evidence to the contrary.   See *C. J.*, 1841-42, pp. 280 *et seq.*

The central authority was disposed to assert its interest in the schools from the first. Nothing could witness this more clearly than the message of the first territorial Governor. On November 12, 1838, he sent his first message to the Legislative Assembly, and his initial recommendation concerned the welfare of the schools. He urged that a law be passed immediately for the organization of townships and the election of township officers, for " without proper township regulation," he said, " it will be extremely difficult, if in fact not impracticable, to establish a regular school system." And later on in his message the Governor was not entirely ingenuous when he announced, " There is no subject to which I wish to call your attention more emphatically than the subject of establishing . . . a well digested system of common schools." When preparing the message he had told his private secretary that the prime object of that recommendation was to attract settlers, and had acknowledged that the territory was not ready for and not in need of a school system.[1] However, the recommendation was taken at its face value, and with at least equal good faith the first Legislative Assembly proceeded to enact an elaborate law for a system of school officers and school organization.

The law of the first session made no provision for State or county control; it instituted a condition of remarkable local decentralization.[2] The directors themselves were given the powers of examining the teachers, and were authorized to lease the lands belonging to the district. There was little or no limit on their authority, though they were required to report to the county commissioners. But the act was tentative, and so too great significance is not to be

[1] *Proceedings of Seventh Reunion of the Pioneer Lawmakers' Association of Iowa*, p. 24.

[2] *L.*, 1838–9, *Act* June 1, 1839.

attached to it.   It met a primitive condition.   In a day of
rude beginnings it introduced rude measures.   For instance,
under it taxes might be levied for school purposes " in cash,
or good merchantable produce at cash prices."   Thus it
was not intended to be enduring, and the decentralization
that formed its basis was not a principle, but an expedient.

The next year saw a complete change.   A territorial
superintendent was created and township school inspectors
provided for, to whom were transferred several of the more
important functions previously enjoyed by the school directors.[1]   Under the law of 1839 the school directors might
make application to the county commissioners for the organization of their districts; now the school inspectors were
vested with full power to set off the districts, settle their
boundaries and change them as they pleased, later even to
form districts covering adjoining townships, with the consent of the school inspectors of such townships.[2]   They
were given the power to examine teachers, a power that
was thus, with exceptions of little moment,[3] lost to the
school directors.   The duty of visiting the schools was
imposed upon them.   They exercised a very important
financial function, applying to the county treasurer for the
portion of the school money due their township and securing
from the township collector the funds collected by him for
school purposes, which they then apportioned to the several
districts.   The powers vested in the school inspectors were
in part original to their office, in a slight measure conferred
at the expense of the county commissioners, in a large
measure at the expense of the school districts and school
directors.   The creation of the office was of signal importance, for it meant that the school system was not to be
confirmed in local autonomy, but that a way was to be

[1] *L.*, 1839–40, c. 73.   [2] *L.*, 1846–47, c. 99.   [3] *L.*, 1856–57, c. 158.

opened for what might develop into a degree either of
semi-local or State administration. It proved to be the
avenue to the former, the county administration, a fact not
surprising when it is recognized that the county has played
perhaps the leading role in the political development of
this agricultural and therefore largely rural people.

The township school inspector system was unique in many
ways. If the school inspector was a precursor of the
county school fund commissioner, and so of the county
superintendent of schools, he was none the less a forerunner
of the authority that grew up in the later township district.
And for a short period his powers were susceptible of
becoming quite autocratic, for from 1841 to 1847 he was
under no compulsion save that exercised in the almost casual
influence of the territorial Legislature.

The Territorial Superintendent of Public Education created at this time, an office that was to endure but a year,
however, was not given strong powers. It was rather a
supplementary office, hence its creation did not signify the
adoption of a policy of centralization. The superintendency
under the State government has been at no time so weak
legally as was this. The powers were few.[1] The Superintendent was to visit the schools, issue instructions for the
organization of school districts, provide the form for the
teachers' certificates, though their examination was left entirely to the school inspectors, apportion the interest of the
school fund—a fund that was practically non-existent at
this time—and report to the Legislature. But in the hands
of the man first appointed to this office, the appointment
being by the Governor with the consent of the Council, even
these weak powers were made much of, and the schools set
on the road of progress.[2]

[1] *L.*, 1840, c. 46.   [2] See *S. R.*, 1895, p. 213.

The work necessary at this time was organization of the
school districts, instruction in and interpretation of the
school laws.   In many places school districts had failed of
organization, in many townships school inspectors had not
even been elected, and all because the law was not known
to exist, or, if known, not understood.   A crusade of information and organization was inaugurated by the superintendent, and much was achieved by him in his brief
career.[1]   A little further assistance and authority was
asked, in order to carry the work forward, but the House
Committee on Public Instruction in January, 1842, in the
face of this evident need, brought in a report for abolish-
ment, saying, " This officer, in the opinion of your committee, is unnecessary. They therefore recommend that
this office be abolished." [2]   From the face of the report it
would appear that the superintendent's salary of $250 per
annum was deemed an extravagance.   The office was abolished the month following.[3]

There have been few steps in the history of the State
Legislature more reprehensible than was this.   It was dis-
tinctly a step in retreat.   The result was not decentralization
so much as demoralization.   Under the law abolishing the
office it was provided that the reports of the clerks of the
Boards of County Commissioners, embodying an abstract
of the returns made to them by the school inspectors, should
be transmitted to the Legislative Assembly of the territory.
Hitherto these reports had been sent to the Superintendent.
The effect was simply to render the provision for reports
entirely nugatory and to remove practically all central oversight and supervision, for it does not appear that these
reports were ever made to the Legislature or that, if made,

[1] *S. R., C. J.*, 1841–42, p. 281.

[2] *H. J.*, 1841–42, p. 132.   [3] *L.*, 1841–42, p. 108.

they were ever examined by it.   If the Legislative Assembly exercised any control it was desultory and unmeaning. Not until the State was admitted into the Union was a general superintendency again created.

The greatest harm in this policy, a harm that was scarcely remedied in a score of years, was the check it gave to school organization.   At the moment when every care should have been given to direct the struggling feet all guidance was removed, so that in message after message the stock complaint of the Governors became just this, that because of supineness of school officers, or the permissive character of the laws, or failure to understand them, the districts were not organizing, and the school system was becoming a cause for mortification.[1]   The later territorial Governors, however, did not mention the matter in their messages.   Apparently they had given up in disgust.   But the conscience of the Legislature began to quicken,[2] and before the State was formed there was readiness for reform, so that the provision for the State superintendency was easily introduced into the State Constitution.

To the school system the admission of the State in 1846, the Constitution and the early State laws meant reconstruction, and now until 1857, when the second Constitution was adopted, the school system underwent a peculiar development, a period of growth, but of growth stunted somewhat by the division of interests and responsibilities of those designated to administer it.   In this period the administration of the school fund shared the time of State and county school officers with the administration of school matters proper.   The pivotal point of the school system in fact was the administration of this fund.   Either the

[1] *Gov. Mes.*, *H. J.*, 1841–42, p. 14 ; *C. J.*, 1842–43, pp, 10, 11 ; *C. J.*, 1843–44, pp. a, 10.

[2] *H, J.*, 1845,p. 164.

legislators of the day seemed to have lost sight of the real interests of the schools in their zeal to take speedy care of the beneficence of the National Government, or they thought that here was the vital point of the school machinery, and that once it was put in working order the entire body would move of itself.[1]   So they neglected its other parts.

The school fund as constituted at this time was derived from the public lands, comprising the sixteenth section of every congressional township, an additional 500,000 acres, together with five per cent. on all the revenue derived from the public lands within the State.   The State University had a fund of its own, derived from two sections of the public lands.   As an addition to the general fund the Constitution of 1846 provided that moneys paid as exemptions from military duty and the clear proceeds of all fines collected in the several counties for any breach of the penal laws should be " exclusively applied in the several counties in which such money is paid or fine collected." [2]   Legislation and gifts from the National Government at various times augmented this fund slightly.[3]   The balance of the school revenue was derived from taxation, and until the free school law of 1858 was passed the amount required of

[1] It is quite evident that much more was expected of the school fund than ever came of it.   The House Committee on Public Instruction in 1842 in a report, said that they were " gratified to say that they can see, in advance, means within the power of the Legislature, if properly husbanded to create a permanent fund of an amount which, in a few years, may be sufficient for all objects of a Primary School. " This fund the Committee propose to create by the collection and funding in the hands of the Territorial Treasurer, all moneys arising from fines, forfeitures, and any violations of the penal laws of the Territory, from drifted water craft, lost goods, estrays, escheats, and the portions of money to which the Territory is entitled under the act of Congress distributing the proceeds of the sales of the public lands." *H. J.*, 1841–42, p. 132.

[2] *Cons.*, 1846, art. 9, § 4.

[3] *L.*, 1848–49, c. 99, added all funds arising from sale of water craft, lost goods and estrays, to be paid to the county in which they had accrued.

each taxpayer was to a large extent determined by the number of his children in the schools.[1] Until that time the interest from the permanent fund did indeed equal about one-third of the school expenditure. The importance given to the administration of the fund thus had some justification.

The Constitution of 1846 provided for a State Superintendent to be elected for a term of two years.[2] The first session of the State Legislature, now denominated the General Assembly, provided in detail for this office and for a new body of county school officers called county school fund commissioners.[3] The financial functions of the State officer were quite as pronounced as those of the county commissioners, so that harmony in description might have been subserved had the Superintendent been styled what in fact he really was, the State school fund commissioner. The county school fund commissioner was provided primarily for the local handling and management of the school funds and lands. And until the discontinuance of the office of school inspector in 1849,[4] when the functions of such office were in a large measure conferred upon him,[5] he was little

[1] For example, see L., 1839-40, c. 73; L., 1845-46, c. 11.

[2] The provision as originally introduced by the Committee on Education and School Lands in the Constitutional Convention of 1846, provided for a Superintendent to be elected by the Legislature for a term of three years. *Journal of the Constitutional Convention*, 1846, p. 46.

[3] L., 1846-47, c. 99,

[4] L., 1848-49, c. 99. Until 1847 there had been three school inspectors in each township; by c. 99 of the laws of that year the number was reduced to one.

[5] He was not, however, given the power to examine teachers, or visit the schools. The former power was again confided to the school directors. The latter was exercised by the State Superintendent and school directors. The school fund commissioner's powers were not so arbitrary with respect to the determination of the boundaries of school districts as had been those of the school inspectors, and in some sense they were entirely taken from him. L., 1856-57, c. 158. With the legislation of 1858 the control of the district boundaries was lodged with the school units. L., 1858, c. 52; L. S. B. E., Dec. 24, 1858.

more than a financial administrator. Yet these added powers affected only slightly his real work and the estimation in which he was held. To the end he was held in popular and in legislative regard as primarily a financial agent, and as such was under the cloud of constant public criticism.

Theoretically the relation of school fund commissioner and State Superintendent during this period was as follows: The active management of the school lands and funds was to be undertaken by the county school fund commissioners; they were to oversee the sale of the lands, the investment of the funds and the apportionment of interest among the districts within their several counties; the State Superintendent was to exercise a directory power merely.[1] But practically there were many contradictions in the system.[2] As a single illustration, the State Superintendent was designated as the proper authority for the receipt of the five per cent. fund, and though he was enjoined to apportion it to the counties immediately, and not allow it to remain in his hands, he did not always do this. The endeavor on the part of one super-intendent himself to loan this fund was perhaps as instrumental as anything in putting an end to the system[3] The result was confusion. There was division of responsibility, at one time at least four different classes of officers, viz., the State Superintendent, the school fund commissioners, the State Treasurer and school inspectors, having to do with the temporary or permanent care of some part of the school

[1] *L.*, 1846-47, c. 96; c. 111.

[2] In some cases the proceeds of the county school taxes had been loaned. To correct the results of this misunderstanding the State Superintendent was empowered in all such cases to order that they be refunded. *L.*, 1848-49, c. 59. There was a similar misunderstanding concerning the five per cent. fund.

[3] *Cf.* L. F. Parker, *Higher Education in Iowa*, p. 28, and see *L.*, 1856-57, c. 162; c. 187; *Joint Resolution*, No. 2.

moneys.[1]   This meant uncertainty, and a hazy responsibility
as between custodians.   Then in the accounts of the officers
themselves there was confusion, so pronounced in the case
of the State Superintendent and school fund commissioners
that legislative interference became imperative.

The system of school fund commissioners was assailed
from the outset, and continually by the State Superintendents.   It was costly to the schools, the expenses and pay of
the commissioners being defrayed from the school revenue,
and by that much reducing the school support.   The Governors united with the superintendents in urging a change,[2]
and when it was shown on investigation that many of the
commissioners were dishonest, many absolutely incompetent, that in numerous instances their accounts were inextri-
cably involved or wholly incomplete, that in some cases the
commissioners had accepted purely " ideal " tracts of land
as part of the school domain, or loaned school assets on second and third encumbrances, the State was ready for a
change.   The superintendents had protested as well against
the continuance of their own financial functions as giving
them little time for proper attention to other school duties.
A mere rehearsal of the superintendent's duties in one year
of the period will almost of itself convict the system.   In
1850 the superintendent's duties were as follows : He must
supervise the establishment of schools, lecture in the several
counties and districts, confer with school officers, receive
and file all papers, reports and public documents transmitted
to him, prepare and transmit blanks for reports, attend to the
organization of the University and Normal Schools, make
rules and regulations for the benefit of school officers, con-

[1] And in 1851 the governor was given power to make such regulations as he
might think proper for the protection against waste of the school lands in the unorganized counties. *L.*, 1850–51, *Joint Res.*, No. 32.

[2] *Gov. Mess.*, 1858, p. 7 ; *S. R..* 1850, pp. 169, 170.

duct the official and miscellaneous correspondence, record and report all the proceedings of his office, and " perform generally such duties as may tend to advance the interests of education." These were school functions properly so called. They were performed without the aid of a deputy and with little clerical assistance. Add to them a duty in the selection and sale of the school lands, apportionment of the interest of the school fund, collection and distribution of the five per cent. fund, the adjustment of land titles, certain duties in the investment of the school funds, and periodical examination of the accounts of the school fund commissioners, and it needs no argument to show that not all the duties would be performed, and that many of them would be performed very inefficiently. In the nature of the case a change must have been pending, and it is little wonder that the change when it was made was not merely in the statutes of the State, but that it became a part of its constitutional law.

The most fruitful years in the history of the Iowa schools and the Iowa school administration are the years 1857 and 1858. Then was laid the foundation of the present system. In 1856 a Commission for the Revision of the School Laws, composed of Amos Dean, a prominent scholar and educator, and then dean of the Albany Law School, and the famous Horace Mann,[1] made a report rich in suggestions for betterment. Its most pregnant recommendations were those for a county superintendent of schools, for free schools, and a township district system, measures that were all, with the exception of the last, realized within two years. The township district in its pure form, as recommended by the Commission, was not adopted, but a compromise system, whereby

[1] Mr. F. E. Bissell, afterwards Attorney-General, had been named as a member of this Commission, but did not act. For contemporary opinion of the report of the Commission see *Dubuque Express and Herald*, Jan. 15, 1857.

the original school districts became sub-districts of the
larger township unit, and a single director from each elected
in each of such sub-districts constituted the township board,
secured the consent of the Legislature.

In the Constitution of 1857 it was provided that "the
financial agents of the school fund shall be the same that,
by law, receive and control the State and county revenue,
for other civil purposes, under such regulations as may be
provided by law." [1]   And thus the educational was perma-
nently separated from the financial administration of the
schools.   But one other provision in this Constitution de-
layed for a period of six years the full entrance upon the
present order.   The State was to undergo a further experiment.   The Constitution created a new organ of government called the State Board of Education, a separate and
distinct Legislature for school matters!   It was the introduction of a fourth element of government, a body to which
either the term Council or Legislature might be applied, for
it might enact laws, it might through its secretary exercise
a broad ordinance power, and these laws and ordinances
once promulgated, it could, at the hands of its executive
officer, secure their enforcement.   It is to be doubted if the
colonial or State history of America since the "Fundamental
Constitutions" of John Locke and the Carolinas affords a
more unique organ of civil government than was this.   It
must be placed among the curiosities of modern institutions
where abide the Swiss *Landesgemeinde* or those wrought
by the curious relations of Croatia to the dominant Magyars
in the Hungarian constitutional system.   It will be impossible here to give it the attention that it deserves, for the
reason that it has little significance in the schools.   Yet so

---

[1] *Cons.*, 1857, Art. 9, Sub-div. 2, § 6.   The creation of a state land office at
this time added facilities for the care of the school lands.

eloquent is it of the inventiveness of the political mind of an American commonwealth that it should not go unnoticed.

The State Board of Education [1] was composed of the Lieutenant Governor, who was the presiding officer, with a casting vote in case of a tie, one member to be elected from each of the judicial districts in the State, of which at this time there were eleven,[2] and the Governor *ex officio.* The qualifications for election were made the same as those for State Senators, citizenship of the State for one year, and the attainment of the twenty-fifth year. The sessions of the board were to be held annually, not to continue longer than twenty days, except upon extraordinary occasions, when upon the recommendation of two-thirds of the board the Governor might order a special session. The board was to appoint a secretary, who should be its executive officer, and " perform such duties as may be imposed upon him by the board and the laws of the State." With respect to powers, the Constitution provided, " The board of education shall have full power and authority to legislate and make all needful rules and regulations in relation to common schools, and other educational institutions, that are instituted, to receive aid from the school or university fund of this State; but all acts, rules and regulations of said board may be altered, amended or repealed by the General Assembly, and when so altered, amended or repealed they shall not be re-enacted by the board of education." But it was stipulated that " the board shall have no power to levy taxes or make appropriations of money." A majority constituted a quorum for the transaction of business, but no rule or law could pass without the concurrence of a majority of all the

[1] For the full law on the composition and powers of the Board see *Cons.*, 1857, art. 5, §§ 1–15.

[2] *Cons.*, 1857, art. 5, § 10.

members. However, a law once so passed could not be
disturbed by veto.[1]

The board was not made a permanent body. It was
recognized by members of the constitutional convention and
others that imagination or pure reason, and not precedents,
were the fabrics from which this new creation was made,[2]
and that the experiment might fail; therefore a way was left
open for retreat. It was provided that after 1863 the
General Assembly should have power to abolish or reor-
ganize it, and provide for the educational interests of the
State in any way they should think best and proper.

The purpose of the board's creation, as expressed by its
author in the constitutional convention, was shared by the
majority of the delegates. He said that it was his desire
to take education entirely out of the power of the General
Assembly and put it in the safe keeping of another body
" who will better represent the interests of the people. I
am for putting it into the hands of a body that shall have
no control over the funds, and which cannot possibly be
influenced by partisan considerations . . . their whole and

[1] In the original report made to the Constitutional Convention of 1857, in which
the board was projected, there was no provision for a veto power. But on Feb. 27,
1857, motion was made by its author for an additional section providing that sessions of the board should not be held during the sessions of the General Assembly,
that the Governor should attend sessions of the board, but have no vote, but that
he might exercise a veto power upon " all acts, rules and regulations passed by the
board in the same manner as provided for acts of the general assembly." The
author of the motion explained on request that it should take a two-thirds vote to
overrule. This motion was put and agreed to.   Motion to reconsider was made
on February 27, the mover contending that it should require but a majority to defeat
the veto of the Governor. But in later action all of this was changed and, as a
compromise to an opposition that developed, the Governor was made an *ex-officio*
member of the board without the veto power, but with no limitation upon his right
to vote. See *D. C. C.*, vol. ii, pp. 838 *et seq.*

[2] One member of the convention referred to it as a "new-fangled scheme."
D. C. C., vol. ii, p. 943.

individual attention will be given to the benefit and improvement of the educational system of the State." [1]   The ambition was laudable, but the handiwork was of the crudest. The issues among the delegates in the convention were framed not upon the feasibility of its existence, but upon the definition of its powers and its relations to the other organs of the government,[2] a controversy premonitory of the friction with these organs that was to prove the burden of its history and finally bring about its fall.

The conflict of jurisdiction between the General Assembly and the State Board of Education was under way even before the board met.   In January, 1858, the first session of the General Assembly under the new Constitution took place, but the board was not convened until the December next following.   Members of the General Assembly believed the State to be without a law in reference to the schools, save the provisions of the Constitution.   This threatened the State with the suspension of the schools for a year, and the Legislature, as in duty bound, passed a well-considered school law, under which all the schools went into operation.[3]   The legality of this law was disputed, and on the threshold of the board's first meeting the Supreme Court pronounced it unconstitutional,[4] and declared that the General Assembly had trespassed upon the peculiar province of the board.   It did not state in terms wherein the unconstitutionality lay, but the decision was almost an admission that it was impossible to define clearly the boundary where

[1] *D. C. C.*, p. 751.   The publicopinion of the board upon its establishment and during its first year or two was high.   A newspaper of the day spoke of it as a body whose deliberations " are second only to those of the legislature in their consequences in the State."   *Dubuque Express and Herald*, Dec. 5, 1858.

[2] *D. C. C.*, pp. 39, 40 *et seq.*

[3] *L.*, 1858, c. 52.

[4] *District Township v. City of Dubuque*, 7 Clarke (Ia.), 262.

the powers of the board ended and those of the Legislature began.   It meant that both board and Legislature must tread lightly the soil of this shadowy division line.

The board approached its task with hesitation.[1]   It took up the unconstitutional act of the General Assembly and passed it with slight alterations.[2]   It advised itself of the further needs of the schools, and little by little undertook to supply them.   But if the General Assembly was to be robbed of its initiative it could well be conceived that with a power to alter, amend or repeal it would not handle over-gently the creations of a rival legislature.   And it did not. The power to revise was freely exercised.

The school legislation proceeded until it became apparent that there was little left for the board to propose or the Legislature to recast.   With this another clause of the Constitution came into play, and it was asked, had the people and the constitutional convention tied the very hands of those upon whom they had sought to confer authority? For the Constitution stated concerning the school laws that when " altered, amended or repealed they shall not be re-enacted by the board of education."   It was a curious provision, and one that was held to mean that the board might not twice act upon the same subject, and that the power to alter, amend or repeal should not be held in abeyance or be twice exercised.[3]   A school law once a law was thus a statute *in perpetuo,* and took on something of the formidable in-flexibility of a written constitution.   These conflicts and self-destructive principles and rules, with their basis of un-matured political science, meant the undoing of the system, and, together with the jealousy of the General Assembly towards a competitor in its own field, succeeded in accom-

[1] *Gov. Mess.,* 1860, p. 7.   [2] *L. S. B. E.,* Dec. 24, 1858.
[3] *Report of the State Board of Education,* 1863, pp. 27, 28.

plishing it immediately the constitutional limitation had expired.[1]

Examined with respect to its power as an administrative machine it is apparent that centralization was here carried to an extreme limit, and had the board been cast on clean lines and endowed with powers less irritating to the other departments of government it could have governed the schools almost secure from molestation. For a legislative, an executive and a judicial power were focussed here, a legislative power limited of course by the right of the General Assembly to amend or repeal, and the inhibition of the taxing power and power of appropriation, an executive power that must no doubt serve the Legislature as well as the board, for the power of the Legislature to overrule the board meant no less, and a judicial power that assuredly would have received harsh treatment had it trenched much upon the authority of the courts, but still a legislative, an executive and a judicial power of much importance.

Exercising its legislative power the board, quick to appreciate the school needs, passed laws that had hardly occurred to the slower moving Legislature. Notable among them was the law for school appeals,[2] though of this it had received a hint from the discussion in the constitutional convention, in which the creation of a Chancellor, with power to settle school differences subject to appeal to the Supreme Court, had been mooted.[3] Furthermore it had a model for such a law in the provisions of the unconstitutional act of 1858. Another step in advance was made when it provided for a State Board of Educational Examiners, who might examine and issue certificates to teachers for the public schools.[4]

[1] *L.*, 1864, c. 52. The message of the governor to this session had favored its abolition. *Gov. Mess.*, pp. 4, 5.   [2] *L. S. B. E.*, Dec. 24, 1859.

[3] *D. C. C.*, vol. i, p. 78.   [4] *L. S. B. E.*, Dec. 20, 1861.

The board itself was not an executive body. Its secretary was the only executive officer, but through him the board might execute its will, for by the Constitution he was to " perform such duties as may be imposed upon him by the board," and though it was in session but twenty days during the year, it was, at least secondarily, something of an administrative council. At the beginning of the board's career the Superintendent of Public Instruction still existed, but the office was immediately abolished by the board, largely for political reasons, and the functions were bestowed upon its secretary. Moreover, the secretary was given a wide ordinance power, the board on the passage of its first school law providing, " The Secretary of the Board of Education may make all needful rules and regulations to give efficacy to this law. And should any defect be discovered therein while this board is not in session, which is evidently the result of oversight, and which in his opinion is detrimental to the efficiency of the law, he may supply such defect by a regulation having the force of law until the matter can be acted on by this board. . . . He may also make regulations fixing the powers and duties of any subordinate officer or board when these duties are not sufficiently defined herein." [1] The authority thus conveyed was not tested, for the secretary, fearing he might transcend the power conferred, confined himself to its exercise in only a few unimportant cases.[2]

Finally the board conferred judicial authority upon its executive agent, certainly a remarkable measure when it is

[1] *L. S. B. E.*, Dec. 24, 1858. Though the constitutionality of these provisions was never brought in question, never receiving an important application, it would seem that the board here approached treacherous ground. This amounted to little less than a delegation of legislative power, a power that in the hands of the board itself could be made effective only upon concurrence of a majority of the members.

[2] *Report of the State Board of Education*, 1859, p. 15.

recalled that the secretary was the servant and mouthpiece of the board. Appeals from acts and decisions of local Boards of Directors might be entertained by the county superintendent, and from his decisions and acts appeals might be taken to the secretary, whose decision was final. Disputes involving money claims or contracts alone were excepted; these were left to the courts.

It is to be regretted that the nature of the board was not such that it could have been given a longer test, for while it was weighted with deficiences, its personnel was vigorous,[1] its spirit was sound, and there was much in its plan that if given a favorable opportunity might have proved invaluable in the development of the schools. As it was the schools did not suffer, but thrived under its régime, though this was doubtless due chiefly to the free school law which was now just under way.

With the year 1863, when the State Board of Education was abolished and the Superintendent introduced, the State was done with experiments. Down to the Code of 1873 reactionary tendencies were at work. The Legislature had regained its control of the schools, and seemingly was inclined to let them take care of themselves for a season. The greater local integration of the school system intended by the adoption of the township district was checked, and local decentralization under piecemeal laws grew apace. During this period was begun that series of acts which, by providing for independent districts, though this had, within limits, been sanctioned by the law providing for the township district, by conferring upon sub-districts the right to constitute themselves independent districts,[2] by permitting independent

[1] See *Proceedings of the Pioneer Lawmakers' Association of Iowa*, 1898, p. 77.

[2] See *L.*, 1872, c. 156, *Gov. Mess.*, 1874, p. 13, and *L.*, 1888, c. 61, for illustration. There were occasional attempts to check this movement, but they were of little avail. *Code*, 1873, § 1713.

districts to divide themselves into two or more new independent districts,[1] or on the other hand to combine, or by
other and multifarious permissions too detailed to mention
made the local school administration a patchwork, without
system and without form, a condition that has endured to
the present day in the face of the protests covering half a
century.[2] The powers conferred upon the State Superintendent were not fully commensurate with those which the
Secretary of the Board of Education had exercised;[3] the
Board of Educational Examiners though patently weak was
not altered, the county superintendents were stripped of
their power of visitation, though this was restored again
within a few years,[4] and a general spirit of legislative indifference prevailed.

But with the year 1870 a lively interest began in school
affairs, and from then on there has been a steady progression
in the expansion of the State and county administration.
The powers of the school directors have remained practically stationary, only a mite of added authority occasionally
falling to them in the laws of general application.[5]

The enhancement of the county administration has meant
almost entirely the extension of the county superintendent's
powers.[6] On the other hand the increase of the strength

[1] *L.*, 1878, c. 133.

[2] The Secretary of the Board of Education in 1858 was in favor of carrying the
change to the extreme of a county district.

[3] *L.*, 1864, c. 52.

[4] *L. S. B. E.*, Dec. 24, 1859, omitted provision for visitation; *L.*, 1864, c. 102,
restored it.

[5] *L.*, 1886, c. 1, concerning instruction in physiology and effects of stimulants and
narcotics; *L.*, 1900, c. 109, teaching of vocal music; *L.*, 1902, c. 128, compul-
sory education. In the light of the history of other States grave doubts may be
entertained as to the success of local administration of the latter law.

[6] The chief additions to the county superintendent's powers and duties since
1863 are found in acts making him president of county high school board, *L.*,

of the State administration has taken several forms. The Superintendent's powers have been increased.[2]   At the same time various special boards have been created with wide functions, and certain extra-legal bodies have developed whose administrative influence is none the less real because unstatutory.   The particular directions in which the several branches of the school administration were strengthened will appear in the discussion of the present system.

In concluding this historical sketch we may summarize and more succinctly indicate the dominant tendencies which have served to stamp the several stages in the school administration.   From 1838 to 1841 we note quite perfect decentralization, almost entirely theoretical however, for the

---

1870, c. 116; requiring him to make reports concerning blind, *L.*, 1870, c. 31 ; deaf and dumb, *L.*, 1874, c. 213; and feeble-minded, *L.*, 1882, c. 40; erect school districts from territory in adjoining counties, *L.*, 1870,'c. 94; appoint appraisers in condemnation of school-house sites, *L.*, 1870, c. 124 (recalling the power possessed by him under the State Board of Education laws to examine sites and plans of school houses about to be built, and give instructions, see *L. S. B. E.*, Dec. 24, 1858); act as arbitrator between local boards, as to where children shall attend school, *L.*, 1878, c. 41 ; making him chairman of county Board of Education, *L.*, 1890, c. 24 ; giving him power to subpœna witnesses and compel their attendance in appeal cases, *Code*, 1897, § 2821.

[1] The more important additions to the State Superintendent's powers and duties have been found in acts providing for a deputy superintendent, *L.*, 1868, c. 115 ; requiring State Superintendent to meet county superintendents in convention, and to visit teachers' institutes, *L.*, 1868, c. 162 (rather a recurrrence to former power that had since been abolished); making him chief of State Board of Educational Examiners, *L.*, 1882, c. 167 (though the State Superintendent's powers were not as great as he had recommended they should be, see *S. R.*, 1877, p. 7); making him president of the Board of Trustees of State Normal School, *L.*, 1882, c. 64 ; giving power to approve courses of study of graded or union schools, *Code*, 1897, § 2776 ; giving authority to prepare and publish courses of study for rural and high schools, *L.*, 1900, c. 94 ; giving authority to appoint substitutes where county superintendent fails to make report, *L.*, 1900, c. 94 ; making him member of the Board of Library Trustees, *L.*, 1872, c. 184.   There was a diminution in authority in 1864, when the power to direct what books should be used in the schools was taken away, *L.*, 1864, c. 52.

schools had not developed at this time. The year 1841-
1842 was signalized by the creation and abolition of the
territorial superintendency, an office weak in legal authority,
hence not indicative of the legislative approval of central
power, but strong in the pioneer enthusiasm of its incumbent. From 1842 to 1847 the territory reaped the fruits of
its Legislature's folly. The Superintendent gone, there
being no county authority to aid or control, the schools were
near collapse, and disorganization was the order of the day.
This was a period of decentralization, of a peculiar type,
however, for it traveled under the guise of a legislative administration. Just above the district was the township
inspectorship, an office that contained the seeds of strength
but did not flourish because of the perverse conditions with
which it was surrounded. The admission of the State
in 1846 meant a new era, and in 1847 great strides were
made toward the centralization of the school system. The
State Superintendent was provided with powers concerning the schools and school finances, which, read on paper
only, exceeded anything that has existed since the abolition of the Board of Education.[1] But in reality the
centralization was not all that it seems, and was in fact
essentially less than what now exists in the State. This
contradiction of appearances and truth is explained by
two facts. First we note the attempt to make the State
Superintendent strong beyond his power of efficient endurance. To give him the power of comptroller of the school
funds, the duties of a register of a State land office and the

---

[1] In 1853 the State Superintendent was made President of the Board of Overseers of the Blind Asylum, which was then established. *L.*, 1852–53, c. 26. Two
years later, however, it was provided that the members of the board should
elect their own president, though the State Superintendent remained for a time an
ex-officio member of the board. *L.*, 1854–55, c. 56. As early as 1849 the State
Superintendent had been required to exercise ministerial functions with regard to
the deaf, dumb and blind. *L.*, 1849, c. 121.

multitudinous functions of director of the school system in all its ramifications, without at the same time providing a sufficient body of assistants, was to insure at the outset that almost none of his work would be done satisfactorily, that much of it would be done poorly, that some of it would not be done at all. The other fact is found in the conditions of the day. The school population was not of any extent until about 1854; the ability of the people to support a school system was very limited. Most eloquent of the times was the provision for the normal schools of 1848—a vision of the law that was not even in part realized for thirty years.

It is difficult to characterize the period from 1858 to 1863, that of the rule of the Board of Education. It is a period of centralization, but centralization so unlike anything found in our State governments generally, or in the history of Iowa before or since that time, that it must be examined by itself and as an anomaly.

The period since 1863 is divided roughly at the year 1870, the years from 1863 to 1870 being marked by a slight reactionary tendency, those from 1870 on by a slow and even gathering of new forces in the county, and more especially in the State administration. The increase of control in the county takes but one form, that of added power to the county superintendent, while the State administrative power develops simultaneously in the State Superintendent and the State Educational Boards.

II THE ADMINISTRATION OF THE SCHOOL UNIT

To make clear the present administration of the schools it is necessary to describe briefly the character of the local administrative division, and the powers of the electors and the school directors in that division.

Since the year 1858, when the township district was adopted, it has been impossible to speak accurately of the school unit as a school district in Iowa, for so various, even whimsical, have been the changes since that time that to-day not one, but three forms of the local school division are found, while the change from one form to another, under the statutes, may be made with such facility that almost all idea of uniformity and continuity is destroyed.   These three forms are named by the recent law "school townships," " independent school districts " and " rural independent school districts." [1]   The chief distinction between the school townships and the independent districts is that the latter constitute entire units, in which the directors are elected at large, while the former are each made up of two or more sub-districts, with the directors elected one from each sub-district, except in those cases where, there being but two sub-districts to the school township, an additional director is provided for, elected by all the school electors of the school township.   In the school townships the directors are elected for a term of but one year, in the independent districts for a term of three years.   The differences between the rural and other independent districts are chiefly those due to differences in urban and country life.   As an illustration, the urban district boards are larger than the rural, and petitions to rural boards may be signed by a smaller number than those to the urban.   The principle of this system, if principle it may be said to have, is adaptability to local preferences.   To say that the principle should be described as adaptibility to local needs would be to defend it, a thing that would require vast hardihood in the face of the years of unbroken condemnation from those versed in school affairs and school government.   This adaptability to local preference has been an evolution; it was only gradually worked out in all its elasticity by the legislation of forty

[1] *Code*, 1897, § 2744.

years, and as though each aberrant contribution were a gem in the system all have been carefully set in the latest code.

The first reports of the county superintendents following the Code of 1897 showed that there were 70 independent and 263 sub-districts having an attendance upon the schools of less than 5; 502 independent and 2,075 sub-districts having an attendance of less than 10; 1,273 independent and 5,100 sub-districts having an attendance of less than 15, and 1,950 independent and 7,379 sub-districts having an attendance of less than 20. In the total of independent districts and sub-districts 53 per cent. of the independent districts and 79 per cent. of the sub-districts had an average daily attendance of less than 20; 34 per cent. of the independent and 54 per cent. of the sub-districts had an average daily attendance of less than 15, and 13 per cent. of the independent and 22 per cent. of the sub-districts had an average daily attendance of less than 10.[1] The arguments against the small district system are platitudes, and so familiar that they need not be rehearsed here. But the above figures, though illustrating only a single phase of the deficiencies of the system, must plead forcibly for the enduring vitaliy of these arguments. There have been, in the last General Assemblies, some indications of dissatisfaction with the system; the movement to bring school advantages to a higher plane through concentration, as in the proposals for transportation of children, and the desire strongly manifest on occasion to provide higher or graded schools for the townships,[2] have been seriously baulked by the minute school division. It may be that the appreciation of these wider educational responsibilities will accomplish what strenuous protest has failed to, and place the system on a more rational basis.

[1] S. R., 1899, pp. 69, 70.   [2] S. R., 1899, p. 19; 1901, pp. 15, 16.

The powers of the electors in the school unit are very inclusive, and were they exercised the electoral administration of the schools would be conspicuous. It needs hardly to be said, however, that they are little used. They embrace the following, viz.: power to direct a change of text-books regularly adopted; to direct sale or distribution of any property, including school houses and sites, and determine the application of the proceeds; to introduce new branches of study; to govern the board of directors with respect to the use of the school buildings for public meetings; to direct the transfer of any surplus in the school-house fund to the teachers' or contingent fund; to authorize the board to provide roads for access to the school houses; to vote school taxes; and finally, as a last principal power, to determine upon the provision of free text-books.[1]

The directors are in a measure servants of the electors of the school unit, and to a slight degree of the county superintendents and the State Superintendent. At the same time they have a certain independence; they may prescribe courses of study, subject, however, to a degree of control previously indicated as existing in the hands of the State Superintendent or the electors; they have control of the school property, may fix school house sites, determine the number of schools to be taught, divide the corporations into wards or other proper divisions, determine the length of time the school shall be taught beyond the period required by law, establish higher or graded and union schools, expel students, visit the schools, and make contracts with teachers and discharge them on investigation. It is apparent from the recitation of the powers of electors and directors that the schools are administered chiefly in the school unit. But

[1] *Code*, 1897, § 2836. The law for district and county uniformity of text-books was not enacted until 1890, c. 24; that for free text-books not until 1896, c. 37.

it will be shown that the external control is by no means a mean or unavailing thing.

III   THE COUNTY SCHOOL ADMINISTRATION

The county school administration is the county superintendent. He is elected by the electors of the county for a term of two years. There is indeed a Board of Education, the object of whose existence is to afford a means for the introduction of county uniformity in text-books, but its power is entirely restricted to that purpose, and even here the county superintendent may become, and doubtless usually is, the guiding spirit, for he is the executive head of the board, with certain sole powers. The Board of Trustees of the County High School is again hardly an exception, and this for two reasons, first because the law for such schools has remained practically a dead letter, there being but one county high school in the entire State, and second because, though the board is made up of trustees elected from the county, the county superintendent is by law always its president.

The county superintendent exercises on the one hand administrative powers both ministerial and discretionary, on the other powers that, with qualifications, may be denominated judicial. Of the administrative powers we shall first speak.

The county superintendent comes into direct contact with the local Boards of Directors in a number of ways. First, he is given a general power to see that the school laws are observed. This extends to all the provisions of the school law so far as it relates to the schools or school officers within his county, and to this end he may require the assistance of the county attorney, who, at his request, must bring any action necessary to enforce the law or recover penalties in-

curred.[1] School directors are required before they may
erect a school building to consult with the county superintendent as to the best plan for the building and secure his
approval of the plan proposed.[2] He has power to authorize
a reduction of the period of instruction in any school below
the limit which the law requires before a school can make any
claim for a portion of the school fund, when in his judgment
there are sufficient reasons for so doing.[3] He may, furthermore, appoint appraisers to determine the value of school
house sites.[4] He visits the schools. Moreover, reports of
district treasurers and secretaries in general are made to him,
and not to the State Superintendent.[5] The general nature
of these powers is readily deduced. They are principally
advisory, though there are some elements of direct administration. And, such is the nature of advisory powers, they
carry with them no great coercive strength.

But the county superintendent is not denied some original
authority, that is to say authority that has its first residence
in him. Most important is the power to examine and issue
certificates to teachers. So important is this power and so
essential to the existence of the county superintendency itself
that it has been urged, when transfer of all examinations
to the State Superintendent has been proposed, that to de-
prive it of this power would be almost complete emascu-
lation. For it was argued that power to examine meant
power to control the teaching force and thus indirectly the
schools. The even working of the system is dependent—
so it was averred—upon the continuance of this power.[6]
These examinations are regularly held on the last Saturday
in each month, though special examinations may be held
at the discretion of the county superintendent.[7] The exam-

[1] *Code.* 1897, § 2740.   [2] *Ibid.*, § 2779.
[3] *Code*, 1897, § 2773.   [4] *Ibid.*, § 2815.   [5] *Ibid.*, § 2739.
[6] *S. R.*, 1901, p. 14.   [7] *Code*, 1897, § 2735.

inations are of three classes, examinations for one-year certificates, for two-year certificates, and for special certificates. The one-year certificates are granted to candidates passing examinations in the subjects that are taught in the grade schools; the two years certificates to those who, in addition, pass in several branches that are confined to the high schools, but are still of an elementary character.[1] Candidates for examination in special studies are examined in these special branches only, but it is provided that no teacher shall be employed to teach any subject not included in the certificate.[2] These certificates once granted, the county superintendent still has power to revoke them for any cause that would have justified a refusal to grant the same.

In still another point he exercises an influence over the preparation of teachers. He is required to hold annually a normal institute for the instruction of teachers and those who may desire to teach, and, with the concurrence of the State Superintendent, to procure such assistance as may be necessary to conduct it.[3] He has a financial power here, for all disbursements from the institute fund must be upon his order.[4] These institutes are supported by the teachers chiefly, the State making only a slight contribution.[5]

Whatever the arguments for or against centralization, it must be admitted that the county institute is a good and desirable thing. But the county examination of teachers is another matter. Here the administration is involved.

---

[1] *Code*, 1897, §§ 2736, 2737.   [2] *Ibid.*, § 2736.

[3] *Code*, 1897, § 2738.   [4] *Idem.*

[5] In 1898 the enrollment in normal institutes was 20,784, and in 1899, 20,454. The entire cost of maintaining these institutes was $59,908.86 in 1898, and $60,717.26 in 1899, or a total of $120,626.12. The whole amount was raised by the teachers, with the exception of $50 paid annually by the State to each county for the benefit of the institute fund.

The decentralization of course is not so pronounced as that in the disorganized period of the schools, when at one time the school directors, at another the township inspectors, examined the teachers, systems upon the working of which there is little evidence, and that little unfavorable. But in contrast with State examination it is local control. The comparative value of the system will be examined in the discussion of the State Board of Educational Examiners.

The county superintendent has a further administrative function, acting as the organ of communication between the State Superintendent and the school unit authorities, and he is required to comply with the directions of the State Superintendent in all matters within that officer's jurisdiction.[1] These obligations are in one important respect enforced by the provision that the State Superintendent may appoint a substitute when he fails to make the reports required, and determine the remuneration of the substitute, to be paid by the county superintendent.[2] Similar duties are found in the provisions that the county superintendent shall file with the county auditor a statement of the number of persons of school age in each school township and independent district in the county.[3] This is to provide a basis for the apportionment of the school fund and income from the county school taxes. The duty to report the blind in his county to the superintendent of the college for the blind, the feeble minded to the superintendent of the institution for the feeble minded, and the deaf and dumb to the superintendent of the institution for the deaf and dumb are not related to the school system, and need be no more than mentioned here.[4]

A judicial power has been referred to. This is the power that the county superintendent has to entertain appeals from

[1] *Code,* 1897, § 2735.   [2] *L.,* 1900, c. 94.
[3] *Code,* 1897, § 2739.   [4] *Idem.*

any decision or order of a Board of Directors in a matter
of law and fact, except those for money judgments. The
basis of the appeal is an affidavit setting forth the error
complained of. The appeal must be perfected within thirty
days after the rendition of the decision or making of the
order. The county superintendent's decision is not conclusive; it may be appealed to the State Superintendent, where
the hearing is final. Until 1897 this authority proved in
numerous instances fatally weak. Previous to that time
the county superintendent had had no power to compel the
attendance of witnesses. But in that year he was empowered
to require their attendance and the giving of evidence by
them " in the same manner and to the same extent as the
district court may do." [1] The effect of this appellate authority has been to make the county superintendent not a
judicial officer, but an administrative court of first instance. [2]

While the population of the 99 counties of Iowa ranges
from 7,995 in Dickinson county to 82,624 in Polk, it will
be found in general to be quite evenly distributed among
them, most all falling close to the average of 22,544. Hence
little fault can be found with the system of county superintendents upon the score of unequal division of power and
labor. Moreover, for the duties performed the salary paid,
which is now $1,250 yearly, with such additional allowances
as the Board of Supervisors may make, can not induce much
criticism, though in the past it has been excessively low. A
step has been made also through the admission of women
to the office. While in 1870 there was but one woman in
the position, there were 10 in 1876, 11 in 1884, 14 in 1890,
and 15 in 1896. [3] In 1902 15 women held the position, of
whom three had filled it for two or more terms, and three of

---

[1] *Code*, 1897, § 2821.   [2] *School District vs. Pratt*, 17 Ia., 16.
[3] *S. R.*, 1897, p. 112.

the remainder had been re-elected or had previously held the office. In the point of educational qualifications the office stands somewhat above the corresponding office in a number of other States.[1] But with all this said, the county superintendency is in several points the subject of grave criticism, and cannot be admitted to have accomplished all expected of it.

It has in fact been insecure of its life from the hour of its creation. From 1860 to 1875 a strong opposition developed,[2] and since that time those who have favored the office but believed that it was in need of improvement have often been chary of advising reform lest it be cut off root and branch.[3] The State Superintendents have generally defended it, though not without recommendations for generous alterations,[4] recommendations so radical in some cases as to mean the aggrandizement, though a valuable aggrandizement it may be, of the central administration at its expense.[5] The chief elements of weakness in the office as it now exists are found in its obligations to politics and its short term. There have not been wanting sharp complaints that in many instances the county superintendency has been a mere subject of political bargain and sale or a gate to the tortuous passage of political preferment. This political element unites with the short term to cause one of the greatest wastes in the entire educational system. The election returns for the year 1899 indicate that 46 of the 99 superintendents were entirely new in the supervisory work of the schools, 32 had served one term, 16 two or more terms, and 5 had previously held the office.[6] It takes at least a year for

[1] See *Code*, 1897, § 2734, and increase by *L.*, 1898, c. 85.

[2] *S. R.*, 1873, p. 41. See also petitions on file in office of Secretary of State of the State of Iowa. B-40, 2228.

[3] *S. R.*, 1892, p. 197.   [4] *Ibid.*, 1873, p. 41; 1889, p. 53.

[5] *Ibid.*, 1901, pp. 14, 15.   [6] *S. R.*, 1899, pp. 26, 27.

the superintendent to become acquainted with his teachers
and the conditions surrounding the schools, and the year
remaining is but a brief period to apply what he has learned,
or make for anything in the way of improvement.

Suggestions looking both to the removal of the office from
partisan politics and the saving to the schools of the educational waste have been made. Of these perhaps the most
original is that in a recent school report suggesting that the
county superintendent be chosen by a county board, something after the manner of the choice of city superintendents
by city boards.[1] It would seem that any improvement in
the county superintendency will be but a temporary expedient. With the increased powers of the State Superintendent, the Educational Board of Examiners and the extra-
legal State Teachers' Association, powers that, unless the
signs of evolution are deceiving, will be extended, the county
superintendent seems destined to become more and more
a mere ministerial agent of the central administration, and
if he become that, the narrowness of his functions and the
unendurableness of his service to two masters, the schools
and politics, should make apparent the fact that the office is
by right no more than a piece of administrative machinery,
and that as such it should be so constructed as to be the best
means to the end it serves. When that fact is recognized
will it not appear that the best method of reconstruction will
be to increase territorially the jurisdiction of the office, make
it cover six or eight counties where it now covers but one,
increase the salary and provide a corps of experienced assistants, make this go-between station, in short, an efficient and
admirable part of a well digested school system, working
in complete harmony with the State superintendency to the
perfection of the schools, and to no other end? Thus

[1] *S. R.*, 1899, p. 27.

there will be the passing of the county superintendency and its replacement by a body of able assistant State superintendents, something after the fashion of an idea, rough but suggestive, entertained by one of the Governors more than thirty years ago.[1]

IV CENTRAL SCHOOL ADMINISTRATION

I THE STATE SUPERINTENDENT OF PUBLIC INSTRUCTION

The central control of the schools has not yet reached that point where we can speak of a hierarchy of school officers with one undisputed head.   But so far as central authority is lodged in any one man it is found in the State Superintendent of Public Instruction.   If his power of control is not highly developed, at least his presence in all parts of the school system is well assured.   There is no branch of the school system, no central or local board, county or local officer having to do with the school, over which he has not some influence, great or little.   He touches the schools at all points.   His salary is but $2,200 per annum, and his term brief.   His position, therefore, cannot be expected to be what it otherwise might.   We may divide his powers into those of direction or supervision, the appellate power, and the advisory powers, and examine them thus in order from the more to the less competent.   It will appear, however, that powers seemingly of the first class might in some instances be more appropriately grouped with the third—so much less real than apparent direct administrative capacity do they yield—and that among the advisory powers are some so efficacious as almost to deserve a place among the so-called directory powers.

The Superintendent is " charged with the general super-

[1] *Gov. Mess.*, 1870, p. 9.

vision of all the county superintendents and common schools of the State," but this authority is purely supervisory. He has no power of removal or suspension of a refractory subordinate, so that one disposed to oppose him can do so practically with impunity. But such opposition is almost never met with, and little complaint is heard upon that score. He is required to prepare, publish and distribute blank forms for all returns he may deem necessary or that may be required by law of school teachers or school officers, and, as has been pointed out, the making of these reports he can, in a measure, coerce.[1]

The Superintendent has power to meet county superintendents in convention at such points in the State as he may direct, and the latter are allowed their expenses in attendance upon the convention. He appoints, upon request of county superintendents, the time and place for holding teachers' institutes, and his concurrence in securing instructors to conduct the same is essential. He has authority to make tours of inspection among the schools, but this carries with it no directory power,[2] and cannot count for much when his other duties are so engrossing. It is provided that he shall have power " to prepare questions for the use of county superintendents in the examination of applicants for teachers' certificates," [3] and it might be assumed that this would give him control of teachers' examinations. But such is not the case, and indeed the object of the provision was merely to determine by whom the printing of the questions should be done. And although not one in twenty-five county superintendents fails to use these questions,[4] the papers are still marked by them, so that there is no uniform standard for these examinations.

[1] *Ante*, p. 49, *L.*, 1900, c. 49.   [2] *L.*, 1900, c. 94.   [3] *Idem*.

[4] This statement is made on the authority of the State Superintendent.

It might be assumed with even greater show of reason that the section of the code providing that Boards of Directors " shall have the power to maintain in each district one or more schools of a higher order . . . and may establish graded or union schools and determine what branches shall be taught therein, but the course of study shall be subject to the approval of the Superintendent of Public Instruction," [1] taken in connection with the act of 1900 empowering him " to prepare, publish and distribute, among teachers and school officers, courses of study for use in the rural and high schools of the State," [2] would give him something of an authority to direct the work done in common and high schools.   But while these courses of study are very generally used in the common schools, the high schools mostly arranging their own courses, the actual control by the Superintendent is almost entirely lacking.   And it cannot be expected that a course of study even under a much stricter statute will be carried out, unless there is some means of direct oversight.   This suggests one of the greatest needs of the system at the present time, to wit, a number of inspectors, or superintendent's assistants, who shall keep a careful lookout for the needs of the school and for the shortcomings of school officers and teachers.

From the standpoint of administrative science the appellate power of the State Superintendent offers one of the two or three most fertile subjects of study in Iowa government. This is so because the State Superintendent, sitting as a tribunal to pass upon the acts and decisions of Boards of Directors and county superintendents, acts as an administrative court of final jurisdiction, and because it has been recognized that in this country an administrative court is an exotic.   The regularly constituted tribunals of the Amer-

[1] Code, 1897, § 2776.   [2] L., 1900, c. 94.

ican and English legal systems have so fully arrogated to themselves all powers of a judicial or semi-judicial nature that a rival tribunal attempting to share the smallest part of their domain is bound to meet with their jealous resistance. It is of value therefore to note how such a body has fared in surroundings so uncongenial. The jurisdiction has been worked out through statute, through judicial decision, and partly through its own definition and interpretation of its powers.

The section granting the power reads, "An appeal may be taken from the decision of the county superintendent to the Superintendent of Public Instruction in the same manner as provided in this chapter for taking appeals from the board of a school corporation to the county superintendent, as nearly as applicable, except that thirty days' notice of the appeal shall be given by the appellant to the county superintendent and also to the adverse party. The decision when made shall be final. Nothing in this chapter shall be so construed as to authorize either the county or State Superintendent to render judgment for money; neither shall they be allowed any other compensation than is now allowed by law." [1] As was shown in the discussion of the county superintendent, his appellate power extends only to cases involving the acts or orders of Boards of Directors. It might be presumed therefore that the section above in its use of the words " decision of the county superintendent " meant decision in the cases appealed to him. But the State Superintendent has as well entertained cases involving merely an original decision or order of the county superintendent himself, associated in no respect with with any proceeding of a Board of Directors—for instance cases where teachers' certificates have been revoked or denied. And as

[1] *Code*, 1897, § 2820.

this assumption of authority has not been disturbed by the courts this wider interpretation of the word " decision " is probably correct.   But here the authority of the State Superintendent ends.   If the decision or order is of a Board of Directors or county superintendent the hearing of the State Superintendent cannot be attacked for want of jurisdiction. If, on the other hand, it is a decision or order of a meeting of school electors or county supervisors or other officers, though it involve at a most vital point the school system, it is beyond the appellate power.   Thus it is evident at the outset that the sphere of appellate authority is a ragged one; and if the development of that authority fails to be a full-rounded whole or to lack in definiteness, some explanation is to be found in its statutory definition.

The denial of power to render money judgments is the one element that, more than any other, has differentiated this tribunal from those strictly judicial.   It is, further, the one element that, more than any other, has spared the appellate authority from the active warfare of the courts.   For the courts have felt that, without power to assess damages or find the liability on contracts, the judgment of the superintendents could infringe their authority but slightly.   And the State Superintendents, conscious of the significance of the reservation, have scrupulously avoided any excess of jurisdiction at this point, and in their decisions, their publications of the school laws, and their instructions to county superintendents have emphasized this restriction more than any other.

The Supreme Court has assisted in the ascertainment both of the extent and the methods of the appellate tribunal. And in so doing it has imported into this authority a number of legal forms and technicalities that have given it something the complexion of an ordinary court.

The finality of the decision in matters properly before the

school tribunal has been supported by the Supreme Court, in the sense that no court will review or set aside such a decision.[1]   And the fact that the power has a large element of the judicial character has not led the courts to overturn it as in violation of the constitutional provision that the judicial powers of the government shall be exercised by the courts.   In one of the earliest cases, a case decided in 1864,[2] the question of constitutionality was raised, but the court held that the action of boards and superintendents contemplated was ministerial, saying, " None will claim that the statute, defining and regulating the duties and powers of the school boards of directors invests them with judicial powers.   Their acts and their authority in their nature are ministerial, and not judicial.[3]   The superintendent in reversing the same on appeal is limited necessarily to the same subject and to the exercise of the same kind of power, and when the statute says his decision shall be final, it means simply as a ministerial act."   In later cases, however, the courts have spoken of the power as " judicial "[4] or "*quasi* judicial."[5]

The courts have recognized that the jurisdiction of the school tribunals is to a certain extent exclusive. Usually in those cases where they provide an adequate remedy the courts will not interfere. For example, it has been held that *mandamus* to compel action by a Board of Directors will not lie where the aggrieved party has a right of appeal

[1] *Wood vs. Farmer et al.*, 69 Ia., 533; *Munn vs. School Township*, 110 Ia., 652.

[2] *District Township vs. Pratt*, 17 Ia., 16.

[3] In *Kirkpatrick vs. Independent School District*, 53 Ia., 585, the court said of the school tribunal, " It may, perhaps, be said to exercise judicial functions, but it does so only in a very slight sense.   It is certainly not a court."

[4] *Desmond vs. Independent District*, 71 Ia., 23.

[5] *Rodgers vs. Independent District*, 100 Ia., 317.

to the county superintendent.[1] And a teacher claiming
that he is wrongfully discharged by a Board of Directors
for incompetency cannot, on the ground that the discharge
is void, maintain an action for his salary without first ap-
pealing to the school tribunal.[2] The cases where the courts
have claimed on their part an exclusive or concurrent jurisdiction in addition to those involving a contract or money
judgment, which the statutes have reserved exclusively to
them, are as a rule cases in which one or another of the
extraordinary writs is necessary to a speedy and adequate
remedy. In the case of *mandamus* this finds a further support in the statute itself. The law provides that appeals
may be taken only from a " decision or order," and this has
been interpreted to preclude appeal in case of omission or
failure to act. Here it has been held that *mandamus* is the
only means of compelling action.[3] Where a board exceeds
its jurisdiction *certiorari* has been designated as the proper
remedy,[4] and where the question involves the construction
of a statute conferring power upon school officers the courts
have quite readily assumed jurisdiction either in *mandamus*,[5]
certiorari or injunction. It is at this point chiefly that they
have insisted on sharing authority with the superintendents,
or even restricting their authority. And in this point the
motive has doubtless been more to guard the integrity of
the powers of the courts than to afford a supplementary
remedy; it has been a jealous motive. The statute provides
that the appeal may be taken from a " decision or order

[1] *Marshall vs. Sloan*, 35 Ia., 445.

[2] *Kirkpatrick vs. Independent School District*, 53 Ia., 585. Of the school
tribunals the court in this case said, " It will be observed that they provide a mode
that is exceedingly simple and inexpensive, and yet one which is superior in many
respects to that which could be furnished by the courts."

[3] *School Laws*, 1902, note, p. 86.   [4] *District Township vs. Pratt*, 17 Ia., 16.

[5] *Perkins vs. Board of Directors*, 56 Ia., 476.

. . . in a matter of law or fact." Decisions in matters of fact the courts will little disturb, as most of such decisions are hardly different from those of juries or referees; but they are very alive to any matter involving a construction of the law, for the power to construe the law is the distinctive earmark of the judicial office. On the other hand the extraordinary writs are frequently essential to the maintenance of justice, and as such most beneficial. This is nowhere better exemplified than in those cases where the slower method of appeal would permit the consummation of a wrong which injunction could check in its inception.[1] There are some cases where the courts have indicated that proceedings through the courts would be more appropriate than those by way of the school authorities, without disallowing proceedings through the latter channel. Then there have been cases in which there is little choice of measures, or perhaps little real necessity for the existence of more than one, but in which the courts have none the less defended their jurisdiction.[2] In other States a litigant has sometimes been subjected to a forfeiture in case he pursues a right in a court when a remedy equally expeditious is open to him in a school tribunal,[3] but in Iowa if the right is one which under the decisions of the courts the litigant has full right to pursue in the courts, he is not discouraged from appearing there.

The powers of the superintendents when acting within their jurisdiction are in some respects broad. The courts have decided that in cases of appeal from the action of a School Board the superintendents, State or county, have jurisdiction *de novo* by the appeal, and can enter any order

---

[1] *Hinkle vs. Saddler et al*, 97 Ia., 526.

[2] *Rodgers vs. Independent School District*, 100 Ia., 317.

[3] J. A. Fairlie, *Centralization of Administration in New York State*, p. 42.

that the board could have made in the matter.[1] The State
Superintendent, it has been decided, has the power of cor-
recting mistakes in rendering a judgment in a case before
him possessed by all courts and judicial officers.[2] And
when an appellate tribunal is unable to decide an appeal
because the testimony is insufficient or the transcript of the
action of the board is incomplete, and the facts are not sufficiently shown, the case may be remanded for a new trial,
or for further action by the Board.[3] But in other ways the
power of the superintendents is much less than that of courts
of law. Although the Code gives the county superintendent
power to issue subpœnas for witnesses and "compel the
attendance of those thus served, and the giving of evidence
by them, in the same manner and to the same extent as the
district court may do," [4] it still seems that he has no power
of committal or fine for contempt, and can only appeal to
the ordinary judicial authority for assistance therein.[5] The
county or State tribunals have not been given power to
enforce their decisions. In New York this has been accomplished indirectly by granting to the State Superintendent
authority to withhold a district's share of the school support
in case of failure to observe the decision, or by removal.[6]
In Iowa a person in whose favor an appeal has been decided
has the remedy of a writ of *mandamus* from a court of law
to enforce the appeal.[7] As regards the costs, however, such
a circuitous course is not necessary. If a county superintendent is of the opinion that the proceedings were instituted without reasonable cause therefor, or if, in case of an

[1] *Munn vs. School Township*, 110 Ia., 652.
[2] *Desmond vs. Independent District*, 71 Ia., 23.
[3] *School Laws*, 1902, p. 89.   [4] *Code*, 1897, § 2821.
[5] *School Laws*, 1902, p. 88.   [6] Fairlie, *op. cit.*, p. 44.
[7] *Wood vs. Farmer et al.*, 69 Ia., 533. *Newby vs. Free et al.*, 72 Ia., 379.

appeal, it is not sustained, he is required to enter the findings in the record, and tax all costs to the party responsible. A transcript is to be filed in the office of the clerk of the District Court and a judgment entered by him, which is to be collected as other judgments.[1]

The State Superintendent has contributed to the rules of procedure, the statutes and the Supreme Court decisions not having occupied the entire field. Some of his rules are in mandatory terms, but the greater number are permissive and advisory in nature. Moreover, he prescribes forms for use in appellate proceedings in common with forms for use in school business generally. The rules are to be gleaned from his decisions. For instance, he has decided that appearance at the trial is a complete waiver of notice, that testimony to be legal must be under oath, that testimony unless obviously immaterial should be admitted and given such weight as it merits, and that at the hearing before the State Superintendent parties interested may appear personally or by attorney and argue their cases orally if they desire, or they may send written or typewritten arguments.

There is not a great variety in the matters involved in these school cases. A great number of them relate to selection or change of school sites, another large group to the discharge of teachers by Boards of Directors. Changes of district boundaries are sometimes brought in question, and cases involving the redistricting of townships, and refusals to restore territory or to establish boundaries appear. The suspension or expulsion of pupils and questions as to the corporation in which they shall be allowed to attend school frequently reach the State Superintendent. The foregoing matters relate generally to orders or decisions of Boards of Directors. Those in which a decision of the county super-

---

[1] *Code*, 1897, § 2821.

intendent in a matter in which he has original jurisdiction
is appealed to the State Superintendent relate almost entirely
to refusal to grant certificates to teachers, or their revocation
when once granted.

We may note the character of some of these decisions;
first, those where an act of a Board of Directors is appealed,
second, the case of appeals from the decisions made in the
exercise of the original powers of county superintendents.

In case of appeals from decisions of Boards of Directors
discharging teachers the State Superintendent has been prone
to safeguard as fully as he may the rights of teachers.   He
has refused to admit the validity of a discharge not made
upon full and fair investigation; he has decided that a teacher
may not be discharged at a special meeting called for the
purpose of securing a modification of his contract.   In the
selection of a site, when a board violates law or abuses its
discretionary power, its action has been reversed on appeal
and the Superintendent has himself undertaken to determine what the intent of the school electors was concerning
the location of a site and issue his order accordingly.   The
right of the board to provide and enforce a course of study
has been determined in its favor.   It has been held that an
appeal may be taken from the decision of the board to place
a petition on the table.   Boards attempting to exercise
jurisdiction over children after the termination of the
school year have been declared to have exceeded their
powers.   And where the right of a teacher to punish a child
has come before the State Superintendent he has held that
the right of the parent to restrain and coerce obedience in
children applies equally to the teacher or to any one who
acts *in loco parentis*.   The conclusion from this decision
has been that the teacher may inflict corporal punishment.
This decision of itself is sufficient to indicate that the appellate power of the superintendent is of real significance.

Although the rendering of judgments for money and, consequently, judgments on contracts, are prohibited to the school tribunals, the decision of a county or State Superintendent does in fact sometimes determine the direction of a money payment.   For instance, it has been held that an appeal from the action of directors in apportioning the assets and liabilities of new districts may be taken, and the final judgment of the county superintendent be enforced by action.[1]

The power of the State Superintendent to review the action of a county superintendent in refusing to grant or in revoking a certificate is remarkable, because only by broad construction can it be inferred from the law, and because it grants him a power which the courts themselves have refused to exercise.[2]   Once an officer has exercised his discretion a court will not interfere with it; it will only compel him to act, and " the power of the court is at an end when the officer has acted, however wrongfully [*sic*] his action may be, in the opinion of the court." [3]   The State Superintendent, however, has made it necessary that in ordinary circumstances at least the county superintendent shall be appealed to for a rehearing before the decision can be carried to him for review.[4]   And it may be said that the State Superintendent would refuse relief unless there had been an evident abuse of discretion on the part of the county superintendent.   Among other cases in which the county superintendent's power to act has been adjudicated is one deciding that he may refuse to enroll such persons as members of a normal institute as he has reason to believe are morally deficient.   The remainder of the cases are of minor importance.

An examination of the cases decided by county superin-

[1] *Independent School Dist. vs. Independent School Dist.*, 45 Ia., 391.

[2] *Bailey vs. Ewart*, 52 Ia., 111.   [3] *Idem.*   [4] *School Laws*, 1902, p. 90.

tendents during the last thirty years makes it apparent that there has been a gradual falling off in numbers. In 1873 there were 179, in 1877, 123, in 1881, 107, in 1885 and 1886 a slight increase, there being 110 and 114 respectively for these two years, but from 1886 down to 1891 there was a steady diminution, as follows: 1887, 96; 1888, 77; 1889, 65; 1890, 48. In 1891 the number shot upward to 78, but the decline began almost immediately, and during the five years from 1896 to 1902 there was an average of about 45. a year. The cases carried up from the county to the State Superintendent in recent years have numbered less than half those decided in the counties. This marks at least one advantage in the system of inferior and superior tribunals. It tends to arrest a large number of cases of lesser importance at the first decision, and so relieve the State Superintendent of what otherwise might be an excessive burden. The falling off in the number of cases may be explained in part by the fact that as the country has been settled and the school boundaries and sites fixed the possibility of disputes on these points has materially lessened. The tendency of the county superintendents to advise against appeals, and the little time they have to give to them, have no doubt also contributed to their reduction, while the alternative processes at law which the courts have gradually offered to the discontented have probably attracted many cases that otherwise might have gone to swell the superintendents' lists.

Another important phase of the operation of the system is found in the affirmance or reversal of county superintendents' decisions by the State Superintendent. Of those cases deemed of sufficient importance to find a place in the published school laws, not all cases appearing there, as the State Superintendent in preparing such laws is given power to exclude such as he deems of little moment, the majority have been reversals. Of the twenty-eight decisions reviewed by the State Superintendent from January 1, 1898, to October 1, 1899, thirteen were affirmed, two modified and affirmed, five reversed, three reversed and remanded, two dismissed, two remanded, and one, a petition for rehearing, denied. It is evident from these facts that the State Superintendent exercises a vigorous independence in his decisions, and is not disinclined to reverse an inferior officer whenever it may seem to him necessary, or on the other hand to adapt the decision to the equities of the case. This bespeaks the need of the superior tribunal, for apparently injustice would be done without it. And so frequent are the modifications and reversals that it is matter of surprise perhaps that it is not taken greater advantage of, and the number of appeals to it increased.

From this partial analysis of the work and operation of the appellate system it is apparent that it contributes very largely to the strength of the State superintendency, and in a measure at least to that of the county superintendency. The knowledge that in a certain large class of questions the State Superintendent may alter their decisions, perhaps entirely disallow them, will make a Board of Directors careful how it proceeds, and will compel it to look beyond the horizon of its own narrow authority to see how the schools work elsewhere in the State, and, with care that otherwise might not be exercised, examine what is law and justice in school administration. This must make toward uniformity in the schools and the development of a feeling of compactness, mutual reliance and helpfulness, and the spirit of organization. Furthermore, the liability of the county superintendent to see his order overturned will make him reflect before he refuses a certificate, and will greatly guard the schools in the county from administration for personal ends or ulterior motives. As much in the knowledge that this power exists and can be brought to bear, as in its actual exercise, does its virtue exist. It is perhaps the failure to recognize this fact more than anything else that explains the criticism of the appellate authority indulged by school officers of the State on several occasions.

In the brief limits of this discussion any attempt to compare the school tribunals with the administrative courts of continental Europe would be futile. But as it is there that the administrative court has reached its highest development the touchstone of their experience should afford some answer to the several difficulties in the school courts of Iowa. And first of all it may be noted that clearer definition of the powers and jurisdiction of county and School superintendents should be made. The words of the Code are only the most general. The results of this are unfortunate in several respects. Such uncertain language has led individuals from caprice and passion to appeal from the decision of a Board of Directors. With no substantial right invaded or denied they have believed that here was a remedy for their private crotchets, and the irascible have so often made demands under this law that superintendents, chiefly because of its too general terms, have on more than one occasion advised the overturning of the entire system.[1] Its uncertainty is, moreover, a great tax on those who are required to interpret it. To arrive at any definiteness of opinion they must not only scan the act, but must search the decisions of previous superintendents, of the Supreme Court, and often the opinions of Attorneys-General. The school law is composed of a written and an unwritten branch, of an administrative and a judicial law. The constitution and statute or code provisions form the basis; these are written, and are both administrative and judicial. The next place

[1] *S. R.*, 1861, pp. 13, 14; 1865, p. 27.

is taken by the decisions of the Supreme Court which, though primarily judicial, embrace many matters confined to the administrative courts in France and Germany. These decisions thus have an important administrative bearing. The decisions of the State Superintendent are entirely administrative. The opinions of the Attorney-General referred to are such as are given upon request of the State Superintendent. Of recent years, especially, the State Superintendent has sought the advice of the Attorney-General, and in some cases, it would appear, quite allowed him to frame the school decisions. In consequence these opinions are given great weight, and often are printed in the school laws as of equal importance with the other matter contained. The two classes of decisions and the opinions make up the unwritten law. Now if the authority of the State Superintendent were clearly defined, and the extent of his jurisdiction detailed by the law, the labor of search and liability to uncertainty would be vastly reduced. Of course under almost no system could entire relief from the necessity of consulting decisions be obtained, but it could be approximated. The incidental benefit that greater certainty would afford to complainants, to Boards of Directors and to county superintendents is so manifest that it need only be suggested, and if the jurisdiction should be made more definite it might with advantage to the schools be extended somewhat. It seems an anomaly that the superintendents have authority when Boards of Directors have acted, but none when they have refused to act. If the State or county superintendent were given power, within certain limits, to perform the functions of such boards when they fail to perform them, there can be little doubt that the directors would be seldom neglectful, and almost never contumacious. And this would not be an entire innovation, for under the township school inspector system the school inspectors, and at some other times the Boards of Directors, were authorized to levy taxes when the school electors failed to do so. When district meetings have acted illegally, without proper notice, or in evident disregard of rights, would it not be well if the school tribunal had some power to grant a remedy? The New York law, after enumerating the appellate powers of the State Superintendent in detail, finally provides in general that he shall have jurisdiction in cases where any person conceives himself aggrieved in consequence of any decision made by " any other official act or decision concerning any other matter under this Act, or any other Act pertaining to common schools." [1] It is not argued that this measure of power should be given the Iowa school tribunals, but it is submitted that some extension would be wise.

The question of enforcement of decisions is closely related to that of jurisdiction. As explained, the superintendents have no power of enforcement, and, except in the case of costs, the one in whose favor judgment is rendered can, in case of non-performance, enforce his judgment only through *mandamus*. Compliance is the rule, but in those cases where it is refused it seems a hardship that a second action should be necessary. There are doubtless a number of ways in which the State Superintendent could be made efficient in this respect without derogating from the authority of the courts. One that readily suggests itself is that of giving the superintendent power to withhold a district's share of the school fund. Although he has no part now in the care or apportionment of these funds, there would be nothing inconsistent in granting him authority to stay their distribution in the hands of the county treasurer until the local Board of Directors had yielded obedience.

---

[1] *Consolidated School Law*, title **xiv.**

The obedience of the county superintendent could be enforced through a power of suspension from office. This would only push a little further the power that already exists to appoint a substitute to make reports when the county superintendent fails.

Again, the organization of the State Superintendent's office in its relation to appeals has been criticised. And there seems a need for almost immediate alteration here. The State Superintendent when a case is brought before him must himself hear the arguments, read through all the testimony and, except as he may be assisted by the Attorney-General, advise himself of the law. His deputy in this, as in his duties on the several Educational Boards, cannot represent him or take his place. The consequence is that he seldom spends less than two, and often more, days in work upon a single case, a part of which might be left to an assistant. If he were given an assistant merely to read through and digest the testimony his labors would be greatly lightened. If in addition that assistant were required to have a legal education, not only would a further burden be removed from the shoulders of the State Superintendent, but the value of his decisions would be increased. Courts of law have their methods of securing assistance in their work. They have their referees and commissions, juries and masters, to find fact and evidence. These aids are incidents of courts; and if the school tribunal, dignified as it is with a final jurisdiction, is worthy of the powers given it, it does not appear why their exercise should not be facilitated.

The advisory influence of the State Superintendent manifests itself in a variety of ways, ways that indicate how generally he has been regarded as an advisory officer. The provision that he shall attend teachers' institutes when consistent with his official duties, that he shall visit teachers' association meetings and make tours of inspection among the common schools, that he " may deliver addresses upon subjects relative to education," and may collect and publish statistical and other information relative to schools and education, and prepare leaflets and circulars relative to Arbor Day, Memorial Day and other days that he deems worthy of observance in the public schools—these powers all attest his capacity to mold the public school system through the force of suggestion and advice. His power to prepare courses of study for use in the public schools is little more than advisory, as is his authority and duty to render opinions on the school law when requested by subordinate school officials. He has been made a member of the Board of Regents of the State University and of the Board of Trustees of the College of Agriculture and Mechanic Arts because of his familiarity with school matters and the consequent value of his advice, from that standpoint, to these institutions. His position on the Board of Trustees of the State Normal School is somewhat different, for he is its president, and so wields an influence more direct than that of counsel. His membership of the State Board of Educational Examiners—so small is that body— also gives him a direct administrative strength as well as a large advisory influence.

There is no other office or officer that touches the educational system in all its parts, no other in which experience with the common schools is made to temper the attitude toward higher education, or knowledge of the internal administration of the colleges of the State sheds its direct light upon the administration of the grades. This is an essential fact in the school system. And it is no less essential to remember that the force which binds the parts together thus in the office of the State Superintendent is not the force of direction or compulsion. It is the milder, and some may say weaker, force of counsel and suggestion.

The State Superintendent has used his advisory influence with telling effect in a number of cases. He has succeeded in awakening a strong sentiment for consolidation of rural schools and the transportation of children. The crusade by him to secure this end was undertaken systematically, by sending to county superintendents and others printed forms seeking full information and free expression of opinion on the matter, by preparation of circulars showing the work done elsewhere in this direction, and the ways in which the experience of others could be adapted to the conditions in Iowa. So thoroughly did the Superintendent disseminate this information, and so skilfully did he make his case, that among the county superintendents, ninety-five per cent. of whom favored the reform,[1] and among a large body of teachers, a strong sentiment for this improvement was awakened. This must mean advancement in the future.

State Superintendents in the past have attempted to aid school districts to secure good plans for their school houses. This has been in response to a feeling on the part of some of the rural districts that naturally he should have in his office a number of such plans to be loaned to districts intending to build. And to meet this need a Superintendent has asked authority from the Legislature to employ architects to prepare such plans and specifications.[2] But this has not as yet been granted, and the Superintendent has done the next best thing; he has secured cuts of buildings already erected,

[1] *S. R.*, 1901, pp. 35, 36. This report, at p. 73, states that " Consolidation has been tried in twenty-eight counties, transportation in thirty-five and both in nineteen. Consolidation has been adopted by sixty-three districts, and eighty districts have transported pupils at the expense of the district. In nine counties districts have been consolidated without providing transportation at the expense of the districts. In sixteen counties pupils have been transported where there was no consolidation."

[2] *S. R.*, 1893, p. 18.

which he prints in his biennial report. The report of 1901 devoted forty pages to this purpose. From 1848 [1] to the present day superintendents have at intervals attempted in this way to fill the need, but with the slight means at their disposal have not accomplished over much. The school houses have improved. In 1861 the log school house began to disappear. In that year there were 893 such school buildings out of a total of 3,479. In 1849 the average value of each of the 387 school houses was $100; in 1860 the average of the 3,208 was $376; in 1874 the 9,228 then reported were worth on an average $892, and in 1892, $1,040 [2] was the average value of the 13,275 schools of that time. Thus there has been a gradual betterment, but a betterment due rather to the increasing population than the dozen or so second-hand plates contained in the school reports. There is place here for beneficial legislation.

The courses for schools prepared by the State Superintendent and sent broadcast over the State have contributed markedly to uniformity in instruction. The inspections, lectures and written opinions of the State Superintendent have all brought information and suggestion to doors where it is avidly received and made the most of. And the Superintendent in his direction of county superintendents' conventions and his acknowledged primacy in the State Teachers' Assocciation has often spoken the word or given impetus to the movement that has resulted in a consensus of opinion, and adoption of measures by school officials that have done as much to improve the school system, to supplement or even fill gaps in the law as legislation itself has done. The State has been fortunate in the character of the men who have held the office of Superintendent. Their opinion has usually carried the weight of high character and strong personality, and in this way weak powers have

[1] *C. J.*, 1848-49, pp. 310, 311.   [2] *S. R.*, 1893, p. 184.

often proved strong and the schools made efficient in spite of legal inadequacies.

We shall not pause here to inquire into the details of the State Superintendent's advisory powers in the several State Educational Boards and bodies. These will sufficiently appear in the discussion of those institutions, and particular examination of the Superintendent's relations to them would make needless repetition.

2. STATE EDUCATIONAL BOARDS

It has been noted in the historical sketch of the school administration that centralization has taken two forms, the first in the increase of the State Superintendent's powers, and the second in the development of State Educational Boards or auxiliary institutions having certain well-defined powers hitherto unknown to the central authority. These boards and institutions have been the State Board of Educational Examiners, the State Teachers' Association, and the Boards of Trustees of the State University, the State College of Agriculture and Mechanic Arts and the State Normal School. We may examine them in the order mentioned.

a　*The State Board of Educational Examiners*

Previous to the year 1861 the examination of teachers, what little there was, was conducted entirely by district, township or county officers. Previous to 1858 it was by district or township officers entirely. At two different periods, from 1838 to 1840 [1] and from 1848 to 1858,[2] it was by Boards of Directors. During the concluding years of the latter period in the particular case of thickly-populated districts provision was made for a special local Board of Examiners, appointed by the Board of Directors, and

---

[1] *L.*, 1838–39, *Act* Jan. 1, 1839.　　　[2] *L.*, 1848–49, c. 99.

consisting of "three competent persons, citizens of said district," [1] who were given power to examine applicants to teach, to issue certificates and annul them, and with the Board of Directors to visit the schools. From 1841 to 1847 the examinations had by law been vested in the township inspectors, but there was much complaint that this duty was not performed by them or was performed unsatisfactorily. The lack of some uniform standard was the principal ground of complaint. County examination of teachers was not known until 1858, though previous thereto a State Superintendent had recommended that the county school fund commissioners should be given this power.[2]

The Board of Educational Examiners of the State as created by the act of the State Board of Education of 1861 [3] was substantially a reproduction of the ideas of the secretary of the latter board in his report to it for the year. He had believed that the Faculty of the State University should constitute the board, because of their "unquestioned ability, and as a matter of convenience and economy." [4] In his recommendation there also appeared the idea, often held in the early school history of the State, that the normal department of the State University should be charged with the highest authority in the preparation of its teachers. He advised that the professor of the normal department should be the president of the board. The board thus constituted was to hold annual sessions of one week, and such special sessions as they might deem proper, at the State University. They were to take as a standard of the qualifications of applicants the course of study required in the normal department of the University, and their certificate—they had but one—was for life. This certificate the board might

[1] *L.*, 1857, c. 158.   [3] Parker, *op. cit.*, pp. 33, 34.

    L. S. B. E., Dec. 20, 1861.   [4] *Sec. Rep.*, 1861, pp. 16, 17.

revoke in case of gross immorality, " or any other cause of disqualification," of which cause the board itself was to be the judge.

The board, like other products of the period, was almost a failure. It was a creation too ideal in nature; the qualifications required were probably too unfamiliar to, if not too advanced for, those who might wish to teach. As a result, during the time this law remained on the statute books, but seventeen persons applied for certificates, eight of whom were rejected.[1]   In addition the board issued certificates, without examination, to persons holding first-grade certificates from some other State and to graduates of the normal department of the State University.

This law was repealed in 1873, and from then till 1882 there was an interval in which the State was without any central examining authority.   A number of bills for a new board were proposed in the interim, and recommendations were made by officials for something to take the place of the venture of 1861.[2]   The plan finally adopted contained some of the features of the old system, but others so foreign to it that it really made provision for a totally different institution.   The old system was imitated by making the president of the State University and the principal of the State Normal School, which had now come into being, members of the board.   Besides these officers, the Superintendent of Public Instruction was made an *ex-officio* member. And two others, one of whom should be a woman, were to be appointed by the Executive Council, neither to be his own successor.[3]

Sessions of the board were to be held twice annually, to be presided over by one of the members, assisted by such

[1] S. R., 1875, p. 127.   [2] S. R.. 1875, p. 127; 1877, p. 67.
[3] L., 1882, c. 167.

well qualified teachers, not exceeding two, as the board
should elect. It was given power to issue two classes of
certificates, first, State certificates, good for five years, which
called for an examination in orthography, reading, writing,
arithmetic, geography, English grammar, book-keeping,
physiology, history of the United States, algebra, botany,
natural philosophy, drawing, civil government, the Constitution and laws of Iowa, and didactics; second, State diplomas, good for life, requiring in addition to the subjects
essential to the State certificate the following: geometry,
trigonometry, chemistry, zoology, geology, astronomy, political economy, rhetoric, English literature and such other
subjects as the Board of Examiners might require. They
were given power to revoke certificates " for any cause of
disqualification, on well-founded complaint, entered by any
county superintendent of schools."

The requirements for the State certificates and diplomas
have remained unchanged,[1] but in other respects there have
been significant alterations and additions of power. The
board has been empowered to grant " special certificates "
to teachers of music, drawing, penmanship or other special
branches, " or to any other primary teacher, of sufficient
experience, who shall pass such examination as the board
may require in the branches and methods pertaining thereto
for which the certificate is sought." Such certificates are
not valid for any branch other than that for which they are
given.[2] Superintendents have also recommended that the
board be given power to issue special certificates to high
school teachers, based upon the branches usually taught in
the higher schools of the State.[3] This has never been done,
however, and would seem hardly necessary, as the high

[1] But see *L.*, 1902, c. 114.
[2] *Code*, 1897, § 2630; *L.*, 1900, c. 96.   [3] *S. R.*, 1895, p. 51.

school teacher's application is usually made a special case
by his employers, and high school teachers as a class are
more and more men or women with collegiate training.

In 1890 the board was given power to issue its certificates
and diplomas to graduates of the State Normal School
under certain conditions. Although at about this time it
was urged that the board should be allowed to inspect,
whenever invited, the courses of study and work done in
private schools and colleges which purpose to prepare teachers, and if they find them satisfactory to grant certificates
upon certain fixed conditions,[1] this power was not granted
until 1902.[2] Under a law of that year schools applying to
the board are examined with reference to course of study,
equipment and faculty, and thereafter an enduring relation
is established between these private institutions and the
State administration, for it is provided that schools so examined shall receive annual inspection by some member of
the board or some one appointed by it for the purpose.
And the principals or superintendents of schools once accredited must file annually with the board a sworn statement
giving statistics concerning the students in attendance.
The board has received a number of applications for such
inspection since the law went into operation, and it is believed that the ultimate result will be to make it the informal
director of teachers' education in all the schools of the State.
This acquisition of authority certainly adds greatly to the
place and importance of the board.

Though under the act of 1861 the Board of the University
Faculty granted certificates without examination to teachers
from other States giving evidence of due preparation, this
power was not given to the new board until 1897. It was
then authorized to issue a certificate or diploma " to any
one holding a diploma issued by a state normal school

---

[1] *S. R.*, 1891. p. 62.   [2] *L.*, 1902, c. 115.

or a certificate issued by a state superintendent or a state
board of education, of any other state, when the same
is in all respects of as high a grade as the corresponding
certificate or diploma issued in Iowa, upon proof of experience." [1]

Complaint had been made at various times, notably in
1895,[2] that the board could not revoke its certificates without the initiation of the county superintendent, the law
allowing such revocation only at the instance of the county
superintendent. The complaint had its effect, and accordingly in 1897 the board was given plenary power in the
matter, and may now revoke upon due notice to the holder
of the certificate or diploma, and after allowing him to be
present and make his defense.[3] The board was strengthened further in 1898 by the provision for a secretary, under
whom the examinations are usually conducted,[4] thus reliev-
ing the other members of a burden of ministerial work.

The number of teachers necessary to supply the schools
of Iowa in 1900 was 18,906. On September 30, 1901, of
the certificates and diplomas of all kinds issued by the board
there were in force 2,365.[5] So something more than one-
eighth of the teachers of the State are examined by the
board. In its history to October, 1901, it had issued in all
3,741 certificates or diplomas, and in addition had refused
a considerable number. In 1900-1901, for instance, of the
1,100 candidates for certificates or diplomas 111 failed.[6]
The number of examinations has steadily grown, and
the evidence is strong that the State examinations are
increasing in favor with the teachers. It has been re-
marked that there is a manifest disposition among them to

---

[1] *Code*, 1897, § 2630 ; and for results see *S. R.*, 1899, p. 177.

[2] *S. R.*, 1895, pp, 51, 52.   [3] *Code*, 1897, § 2631.   [4] *L.*, 1898, c. 73.

[5] Computed from *S. R.*, 1901, p. 189.   [6] *S. R.*, 1901, p. 188.

work first for the certificate and afterwards for the diploma.[1] And the examinations have been not a source of loss, but of profit to the State, the total income from fees at the last report, for the period 1882-1901, having been $12,479, while the total expenses were but $8,928.43.[2]   In every way the State examination is one that may be encouraged.

The preparation of the teachers of the State is not yet what it should be. The county examination is not adequate. It fails most conspicuously in encouraging the higher preparation. In 1900 of the 18,906 teachers necessary to the schools of the State nearly 8,000 had less than one year's experience, while 12,615 in country schools held county certificates of the second and third class, and nearly 6,000 had received only such scholastic instruction as is provided in the rural schools and the smaller cities and towns.[3]   These conditions have been made the basis of arguments for additional normal schools. They as well attest the need for a general raising of the level of the lower examinations, for only in this way will the inefficient teachers be eliminated.   And it would seem that this cannot be done without a greater centralization, without State supervision and direction; for as long as there are 99 county superintendents issuing certificates just so long will there be 99 different standards and looseness and uncertainty of method. And while this system continues unmodified it is to be expected that many county superintendents will be skeptical of the thoroughness of the examinations by their fellows, and will justly resist the registration of certificates issued in counties other than their own. To the argument that depriving the county superintendents of the right of examination would reduce the office to a powerless

---

[1] *S. R.*, 1895, p. 52.   [2] *Ibid.*, 1901, pp. 188, 189.
   S. R., 1901, pp. 17, 126.

position—if that be admitted an undesirable prospect—strong answer is found in the suggestion that while the State board is given the power to issue all certificates, that of vetoing the board's grant in case the candidate lack in moral character, aptness to teach or ability to govern may be reserved to the county authority. It is believed that this is a subject that will not down, that discontent will grow among those who reflect upon the system of examinations in Iowa, and that unless all the signs of the times are false the broad result will be central control of the preparation of teachers and central examination of those seeking to practice their profession.

b. *The State Teachers' Association and the High Schools.*

The State Teachers' Association, though an extra-legal organization, claims attention because it has provided an element in the school administration which in many States is found in regularly constituted officers or boards. This element appears in the determination of courses of study and the standard for high schools.

The term " high school " as a specific description is not known to the laws of the State.[1] And at no time has there been a law which has provided sufficient supervision of intermediate education. The very general power of the State Superintendent to pass upon the courses of instruction in " higher " or " graded " schools has meant almost nothing. Very few courses have been submitted for his approval.[2] He has no inspectors, or other than office assistants. He cannot himself give the time to the inspection of these schools without sacrifice of other interests.

---

[1] *L.*, 1848–49, c. 99, was the first law to contemplate schools of advanced grade. It provided that school directors might establish " a school of a higher grade" in their districts. The law was not of much practical significance for many years.

[2] *S. R.*, 1899, pp. 43, 45, 46.

Failing adequate administrative machinery, the Board of Regents of the State University and the State Teachers' Association have lent a hand. That they have persuaded many high schools to adopt their courses of study has been largely due to the fact that they exercise a real power, that of accrediting such schools to the colleges and universities of the State. Every high school is anxious to become thus accredited, for it is an evidence of fitness.

The earlier work of the State Teachers' Association was rather advisory in character. But it tended constantly to give a definite meaning to the term " high school," which previous to 1873 had signified little more than an advanced graded school, until now it is a more exact description in Iowa than either college or university.

The teachers at various times made rules and outlined courses for high school instruction, and their advice met with a generous reception at many hands. But only gradually have their resolutions been given almost legal force, and become, as it were, a part of the school law. In 1900 the General Assembly authorized the State Superintendent to publish and distribute a course of study for high schools. The State Teachers' Association having for several years been at work through a committee on a manual for high schools, it was thought wise that the school department should co-operate, and the manual prepared by the association was published by the Superintendent. By considering the peculiar conditions and needs of Iowa schools, the requirements for a high school course suggested by the National Educational Association, and the entrance requirements of Iowa colleges, it evolved a thorough plan of instruction. It also prescribed anew rules for the accrediting of the schools.[1] Application is to be made by the proper school officer to the secretary of the committee on secondary

[1] *S. R.*, 1901, p. 261.

school relations, or to the professor of the science and art of teaching in the State University, who is also the official recorder of the committee on secondary school relations representing the college department.   Upon receipt of this application, together with a statement of the high school course, an analysis of the course is made in the office of the official recorder.   After the high school has been inspected and the inspector's report and the analysis of courses have been submitted to the committee on secondary school relations, the committee will accredit the school, if it appears that the conditions required have been met.   It will be seen that the State University, the State Superintendent and the State Teachers' Association are component forces in this movement, but that the regulations are primarily in the name and by the authority of the State Teachers' Association.   If the State is to assume directly the supervision of high school education one of two things will probably be necessary, either the power of the State Superintendent will have to be made more definite, and perhaps increased, and a corps of inspectors or assistants attached to his office, or a State Board of Education created, of whose authority the direction of high schools may be made a part.

3   THE BOARDS OF TRUSTEES OF THE STATE EDUCATIONAL INSTITUTIONS

From the first higher education has been considered a function of the State.   The policy of making it such had its origin partly in the conception of Commonwealth duty entertained by early legislators, and partly in the incentives offered by the United States government in the public land grants.   Other States whose admission shortly preceded that of Iowa had been given lands for the encouragement of higher education, and so Governors and members of the Legislatures and of the constitutional conventions united in the effort to obtain like concessions.

The State University was the first State educational
institution to appear. A law of 1847 [1] provided for its
organization, but it had no real existence until 1854.[2] The
University was discontinued a few years thereafter, but
was reorganized in 1860.[3] The project was cast in an
ambitious mold. Indeed, the sanguine expectations of the
guardians of the educational interests carried them so far
that in 1849 they provided for two branches, which were
in fact to be largely independent, and which, with a hope
of securing further national aid, were given a basis well-
nigh as broad as that of the State University itself.[4] But
the aid was not forthcoming, and the interest flagged until
in the Constitution of 1857 the possibility of three or more
State Universities with three or more Boards of Trustees
was given its constitutional quietus, the Constitution of that
year providing that the University should be established at
Iowa City without branches at any other place, and that the
university fund should be applied to that institution and no
other.[5]

In 1858 the State College of Agriculture and Mechanic
Arts, or, as it was then called, the State Agricultural College
and Model Farm, was established,[6] and in 1876 the State
Normal School.[7] The State Agricultural College was but
the expansion of an idea that had been entertained from the
beginning of the State, and had found expression in the Constitution and the frequent legislation that granted support
to farmers' institutes or in other ways fostered the agricultural interests. All that was needed to bring it into being
was a touch of the right precipitant, and this the offering

[1] *L.*, 1846–47, c. 125.   [2] Parker, *op cit.*, p. 79.

[3] *Report of the Senate Committee of Schools and State University, S. J.,* p.
227 ; Parker *op. cit.*, pp. 86, 87.

[4] *L.*, 1849, c. 114, c. 115, c. 117.   [5] *Cons.*, 1857, Art. 9, Subdiv. 1, § 11.

[6] *L.*, 1858, c. 91.   [7] *L.*, 1876, c. 129.

of public lands by the United States government afforded. The State Normal School was the late fruit of a seed sown at a very early time. An act of 1848 [1] had provided that the State should be divided into three districts, in each of which should be established a normal school governed by a Board of Trustees appointed by the Board of Trustees of the State University; later by the State Superintendent. [2] There were several appropriations for the schools and efforts to put them in operation, [3] but they amounted to little, and until the State Normal School was established in 1876 at Cedar Falls there was practically no State instruction for teachers save that in the normal department of the State University.

These three institutions are, and throughout their history have been, governed by distinct boards that, varying frequently in their composition and sometimes in important elements of their powers, have yet constituted independent administrative bodies under no superior except the Legislature and, in some minor points, the administrative and executive departments of the State government. For a brief period the Board of Regents of the State University was chosen by an educational board, the State Board of Education, and so was in a measure amenable to it. [4] But, as has been pointed out, this board was in school matters the State Legislature for the period from 1858 to 1863, and so the case may be argued no real exception, or, if one, an abnormality, and so unimportant. And not only have these boards been independent; there has been little close relation, even of a consultative nature, between them. The State Superintendent is now a member of all three of these boards,

---

[1] *L.*, 1848, c. 78.   [2] *L.*, 1848, c. 78; *L.*, 1851, c. 74.

[3] *L.*, 1851, c. 74; *L.*, 1856, c. 209. These instances are illustrative merely and do not exhaust the material.

[4] *L., S. B. E.* Dec. 25, 1858.

and is president of the board of the State Normal School.[1]
The Governor has for many years been a member and president of the Board of Regents of the State University.   In
1898 he and the State Superintendent were made members
of the board of the State Agricultural College.[2]   Through
the Governor, then, there is the opportunity for bringing
the State University and the State Agricultural College
into some harmony with the general State administration,
through the State Superintendent of making known to all
three institutions the course that will best subserve the interests of the school administrations, but there is nothing
to compel this harmony.

The board of each institution is elected by the General
Assembly.   The regents of the State University are composed of one member chosen from each congressional district of the State for the term of six years, while the six
trustees of the normal school, having the same term, are
chosen from the State at large.[3]   The boards are non-
partisan only to this extent, that all the members on the
same board may not be of the same political party.   The
presidents of the three institutions, though they have been
members of their respective boards in the past are no longer
so, and thus the administration is entirely apart from the
institutions themselves.

Of the powers of these boards it may be said, in general,
that they extend with little limitation to the full supervision
and government of the institutions.   Among the more
important powers of the Board of Regents of the State

[1] In 1847, when the university was provided for he was made *ex-officio* president of the board, *L.*, 1847, c. 125 ; after abolition of State Board of Education he
was at first omitted from the Board, *L.*, 1864, c. 59 ; again made a member in
1870, c. 87; dropped in 1873, *Code*, 1873, § 1587; replaced in 1876, c. 147.

[2] *L.*, 1898, c. 76.   However the State Superintendent had previously been a
member of the Board for several years.

[3] *Code*, 1897, § 2609.

University are the power to appoint and discharge the president, professors and instructors, to grant degrees and diplomas, and authorize the sale of university lands and the investment of university funds. The Board of Trustees of the State College of Agriculture has similar powers, as also has the Board of Trustees of the State Normal School except that, this school having no special estate or endowment of its own, the board has power merely to make requisitions upon the appropriation of the State Legislature.

The institutions of higher education have prospered under this independent board system; the State College of Agriculture has taken a place in the front rank of educational institutions. The State University is not so prominent, but this is hardly due to any defect in the administrative system. It is attributable on the one hand to the comparative newness of the State, and on the other to the lack, in the past, of generous appropriations. The State Normal School has grown by leaps and bounds, and the pressure for more adequate facilities is becoming strong, many of the neighboring States having three or more such institutions.[1] There is as yet little call for any great degree of centralization in the administration of these institutions. They are still in their formative period. Their character is not developed. And until the full extent of the service that higher education must perform in the State has been ascertained, and the consciousness of the unity of all educational interests has more fully developed in the minds of the people, these institutions will perhaps develop best if left to themselves and their separate boards. But gradually, step by step, it must appear that central advice and central supervision will increase greatly the economy and efficiency of this branch of the school system.

The independent colleges and universities of the State,

[1] *S. R.*, 1899, p. 33.

of which there are now some thirty-one, have been allowed to grow as they would. Legislatures and State Superintendents have ever kept their hands off. And this has probably been the necessary price of their establishment. But now that they have taken root it would seem that the time had arrived for State interference. There are a number of such institutions maintaining a high standard, but many have courses but little above a good high school course. Administrative regulation of charters, and perhaps of degrees and courses, is a remedy needed in many cases.

V THE RELATIONS OF THE SEVERAL BRANCHES OF THE SCHOOL ADMINISTRATION

In the discussion of the present system of administration and its evolution one fact or tendency has stood out above all others. The school administration is not closely organized. It has not been systematized save in a loose and, as it were, concessive manner. We see the school directors and school electors shaping willy-nilly the school unit, to the destruction of uniformity in the foundations of the schools. We see the county superintendents exercising powers which are in other ways exercised in part or participated in by central administrative authorities. The county superintendent examines teachers; the State Board of Educational Examiners examines teachers; the State Superintendent through the board and through his questions prepared for the county superintendents examines them. It is difficult to say just who does examine them. In fact there is no standard test. And these are single illustrations, that might be multiplied, of the nature of the administration. The Legislature in many instances has intended and secured decentralization, in several it has intended centralization and has secured it, in a number it has intended centralization and failed to secure it, in the balance it has intended nothing whatever—so far as consistent relationship of one part to another is concerned—and has secured it.

The common school system of Iowa is theoretically symmetrical. Many Legislatures, school officials, and the courts as well, have contributed to the theory that the system is the common school system of the *State* and not of localities, rising in well-defined stages from the primary, through the high schools to the State University, the State University as well as the lowest grade being part and parcel of the " common school system." There is thus in public opinion the foundation for a well-rounded system of school administration, and that it has not been entirely realized is due chiefly to the bargaining and opportunistic attitude of the General Assemblies and their failure as yet to grasp at one moment all the interrelations and the interdependence of the parts of the school administration.

The centralization of the last forty years has been in response to proved needs. At each addition of power only a part of the school system has been in review, and that part alone affected by the law. Very naturally the result is a somewhat rambling and disjointed structure. Certain definite powers we have seen are already in the hands of the State authority. Conspicuous among them are the power to decide appeals, the power to direct the instruction of teachers in the counties, a measure of authority in the examination of teachers, in the prescription of courses for the high schools, and the decentralized State control of the State's higher educational interests. But it is in the indefinite, the as yet not fully realized powers, that the progress of the tendency toward centralization is most prominently marked. Authority has been brought up to the State capital under a veil. It may not be announced for five, for a score of years, but it is there, and all that is needed is the signal which shall cause the veil to fall and the power to be proclaimed. The power of the State Superintendent to publish the courses for the common schools; this with the change of a word or two will bring the power to direct, to a large extent, the observance of these courses. His power to pass upon courses in higher schools awaits only the provision for assistants in his office to render it effective. His power to appoint substitutes when county superintendents fail to make reports is the next step to the power to appoint substitutes when they fail in any of their duties. It is very near to the power of removal. The ever increasing authority of the Board of Educational Examiners to grant various certificates on examination, and its power to revoke such certificates, is probably not far from a complete central control of teachers' examinations. Its authority to inspect private normal schools and accredit them, and to enter into reciprocal relations with other States in granting certificates, clears the way for the assumption in time of almost complete direction of the educational qualifications of teachers. The manual prepared by the State Teachers' Association and published under the authority given the State Superintendent to prepare a course for high schools has created a standard for high schools that once given statutory endorsement may bring the day of State examination of high school students. And making the State Superintendent a member of the boards of the three State educational institutions and president of one of them, and the Governor a member of two and the president of one, has pointed the way toward the welding of all the school interests under one supervisory authority. In fact there is hardly a direction in which some step has not been taken toward central control except in the matter of common school finance,[1] other than the school

---

[1] Of late years there have been some slight indications that the State has been preparing to aid the schools. In 1900 a bill providing for public high schools, which should be supported largely at State expense, passed the house of representatives, but failed in the senate. *S. R.*, 1901, pp. 15, 16.

fund, and the regulation of the independent colleges other than normal schools.

It has been pointed out wherein a change in the school unit has long been desirable. And it has been shown that the weakening of the county superintendency through the strengthening of the central administration will probably necessitate a reconstruction of the county administration. It now remains to ask what changes may be wrought in the central organization?

Since the days of the State Board of Education a general State council of trustees of public education has not been seriously debated. Yet only through an administrative council, a council or board without legislative powers, does the way seem clear for elimination of the wastes of the present system. As it now exists, with its independent boards, there is much duplication and much failure of information, defects that the consolidation of interests would terminate. It is of course to be admitted that the several State educational institutions need particular administration, that is, each needs the care of a body whose attention is devoted chiefly to it. And the common schools above all need direct and special oversight. But these things the idea of a State council of trustees does not fail to find ample room for. It may be made up of a series of boards, one for the State University, one for the State Agricultural College, one for the State Normal School and the instruction and examination of teachers, one for the high schools, one for the primary schools, one for university extension or otherwise, each board practically independent within its sphere. But when matters of general interest, or matters touching more than one board, are under consideration, the council would act in boards united, or a sort of administrative committee of the whole. The State Superintendent may be continued as the executive chief of the council. It is not so much in the organization of this council as the manner of choice of its members that the difficulty would lie. The boards of the educational institutions elected by the General Assembly, and the State Superintendent chosen by the electorate, are now dependent upon party politics. The non-partisan element in the boards is almost entirely wanting. It should be extended. And the manner of choice of the council should be modeled more after that of the Board of Educational Examiners, whose members obtain their place by virtue of educational office or by appointment. The final element should be an increase in the tenure of office. In this way it would seem a State council whose interests were those of the schools, and whose qualifications were those of educational administrators, would be most likely to be obtained.

Since the year 1870 Iowa has stood first or second among the States having the smallest percentage of illiterates. In some points, however, it has fallen below other States. It has paid its teachers lower salaries than many States. Its direct assistance to high schools, to normal schools and to higher education in general has been considerably less than that of a number. But on the whole its educational progress has been remarkable. For this reason the advocacy of betterments might seem impertinent were it not remembered that the upward tendency of the State, its striving for improvement, is a constant invitation to such recommendations. The State has claimed the schools as its own. Almost unconsciously it has by gradual degrees brought them nearer perfection. All that is needed then is to encourage the movement in the groove that it now follows, and awaken the instinctive groping to a conscious knowledge that what it wishes and is aiming for is in reality a further development in the centralization of its school administration.

CHAPTER III

CHARITIES AND CORRECTIONS

I HISTORICAL DEVELOPMENT OF THE ADMINISTRATION

THE most important act in the development of the charities and corrections of Iowa was that of March 26, 1898. This act at one stroke consummated the centralization of the control of State institutions, under the Board of Control. Only second in importance was the act of April 7, 1900, which provided that the Board of Control should have power to inspect and supervise local institutions, county or private, in which insane persons are cared for. This law marked the first step toward the central direction of local administration in this department.

The local administration of charities and corrections falls into two clearly defined periods, the first extending from the beginnings of government in Iowa to the act of 1900. During this period the locality was left to its own devices, unmolested by any State official. In 1900 the first step toward centralization was taken. From one viewpoint, however, it may be said that with the granting of State aid to special classes, and the establishment of the State charitable, reformatory and penal institutions, a decided departure from local administration was made, for the State thus assumed functions that otherwise must have developed to a greater or less extent in the local divisions.

The administration of the State institutions as well evinces two chief periods, that from the foundation of the institutions to 1898, a period of large administrative independence; that from 1898 on, a period of administrative dependence upon the central board. But in this case there is the lively suggestion, at least, of a third period, a period of agitation and transition with elements of limited centralization. This period begins in 1870 and extends to 1898.

Though central and local administration in these matters are closely related, it will conduce to clearness in the description of their development in Iowa if the two are distinguished and discussed somewhat apart.

I. DEVELOPMENT OF THE LOCAL ADMINISTRATION

The local public administration of charities in Iowa has been confined to poor relief, and, largely as an incident thereto, the care of the insane. There have been certain private charities for special classes, but they are special classes of the poor, usually orphans, sometimes the aged, rather than any who by reason of an unusual physical infirmity, other than insanity, need distinctive aid. The care of the blind, of the deaf and dumb, and of the feeble-minded has ever been assumed by the State. Local correctional or reformatory administration is lacking, while that of a punitive character is confined to the prisons and jails.

Save for a period of hesitation in the early territorial laws the obligation for the support of the poor has been with the counties. The laws of Wisconsin, under which Iowa, at least nominally, had been administered, provided for county relief.[1] The first session of the territorial Legislature failed to provide for the creation of townships, and only indirectly referred to a pauper class, mentioning it in a law [2] concerning the management of affairs of insane persons. The laws of the second session provided for

---

[1] *Laws of the Territory of Wisconsin*, 1836–38, p. 128.

[2] *L.*, 1838–39, Jan. 19.

county support.[1]   There was also legislation for township
organization.[2]   The township officers were numerous, and
among them were two overseers of the poor.   The second
session following, an act was passed which tended to throw
the responsibility for poor relief into confusion.[3]   Its effect
was apparently to make the township itself liable for all
paupers of doubtful settlement, the directors of the poor of
the county having power to reject the pauper if they believed he had not gained a settlement in the county.   This
was out of harmony with the policy of county responsibility.
And it is probable that the Legislature exceeded its intention, for within two years it expressly repudiated the law
and made the provisions for county obligation unequivocal.[4]

One of the significant features of these early laws is found
in the multiplication of offices.   There were to be special
directors for the county poor houses,[5] though in financial
matters they were amenable to the county commissioners.
However, when in 1851 the county judge was made the
county administrative authority, his direction of the administration of the poor relief was practically absolute.[6]
In 1860 when he was succeeded by the Board of Supervisors the management of poor relief was not detached, but
made a part of the central county administration.[7]   Even
in the townships in the earlier period there was a double set
of officers, the overseers of the poor and the township trustees, checking each other in the poor administration, a system that endured for something less than five years, when
in 1845 the township trustees were made by virtue of office
both overseers of the poor and fence viewers.[8]

From the final lodgement of responsibility for care of the

[1] *L.*, 1839–40, c. 59.   [2] *L.*, 1839–40, c. 39.   [3] *L.*, 1841–42, c. 67.
[4] *L.*, 1843–44, c. 12.   [5] *L.*, 1841–42, c. 93.   [6] *Code*, 1851, § 828.
[7] *L.*, 1860, c. 46.   [8] *L.*, 1845, c. 11.

poor with the counties to the year 1900 there was little
change of significance. The autocratic authority of the
county judge from 1851 to 1860 and the tendency later
developed to accord township and city officers greater freedom in the relief of the poor are the two most noteworthy
facts.

The county judge had power to appoint the directors of
poor relief, one or three, as he should see fit.[1] In case the
ordinary revenues of the county proved insufficient for the
expenses of the poor house he might, as a court, levy a tax
not exceeding one mill on the dollar.[2] The reports of the
directors were to be made to him.[3] And he might let out the
support of the poor with the use of the poor house and farm
for a period not exceeding three years.[4] One rather remarkable provision of the law was that creating a system
of secret espionage in cases of special contract for the support of the poor. It was provided that the county judge
should appoint some person to examine from time to time
and report upon the manner in which the poor were kept and
treated, without notice to the person contracting for their
support.[5]

The early acts chartering cities sometimes provided for
city infirmaries. In 1868 city councils of cities of the first
class and township trustees were required to provide for
the relief " of such poor persons * * as should not in
their judgment be sent to the county poor house," for which
a sum not exceeding two dollars per week, exclusive of
medical attendance, might be allowed. But the Board of
Supervisors had power to limit the amount of the relief
furnished and refuse to continue such relief.[6] Thus a limited authority was given townships and cities in the matter

---

[1] *Code*, 1851, § 828.   [2] *Ibid.*   [3] *Ibid.*   [4] *Ibid.*, §§ 847, 825.
[5] *Ibid.*, § 826.   [6] *L.*, 1868, c. 95.

of out-door relief, and from this time on there was a series of laws providing for slight modifications of the system.[1]

The administration of the jails throughout the history of Iowa has been entirely in the hands of local officials. And there has been practically no agitation at any time for central control or inspection. The laws, if observed, however, have usually been rigid enough to secure a good administration. The earliest territorial law on the subject made it unlawful for sheriff or jailer to confine male and female prisoners, except husband and wife, together,[2] and in 1843 any person having the care of any jail allowing it to become foul or unclean, so as to endanger the health of any prisoner, was made liable to indictment and fine.[3] Oppression of prisoners was most severely punished.[4] These provisions have since been extended.

The Code of 1851 took a step forward. It provided for county inspection of jails, the inspection to be made by the county judge and the prosecuting attorney.[5] The provision for a thorough examination of the jails was very full, and it might have seemed that here was the first step toward central supervision. But not so, for when the county judgeship was abolished in 1868 [6] his functions were transferred to the circuit judge, and the Code of 1873 expressly provided that the circuit judge and district attorney should be inspectors of jails.[7] The circuit judge disappeared, but his disappearance was not taken advantage of to create a State prison board, and the system of 1851 is to-day continued substantially in the provision of the law which makes the clerk of the district court and the county attorney inspectors of the jails.[8] These laws in many cases are practically dead

---

[1] L., 1826, c. 26; 1878, c. 37 ; 1880, c. 133; 1888, c. 101; Code, 1897, § 733.

[2] L., 1838–39. c, 139.   [3] Compiled Statutes, 1843, c. 49.   [4] Idem.

[5] Code, 1851, § 3110.   [6] L., 1868, c. 86.   [7] Code, 1873, § 429.

[8] Code, 1897, § 5645.

letters, and seemingly in several periods the Legislature has been careless of providing any system of prison inspection whatever.

Thus to the year 1900 in both local charity administration, with its incident of the care of the insane, and in the management of jails, the control was left wholly to county or lesser hands. But in this year there appeared a most important deviation. The General Assembly enacted a law providing that all private and county institutions caring for insane persons should be under the supervision of the Board of Control of State Institutions.[1] This law imposes upon the board the duty of inspecting such institutions through its own members or persons appointed by it. This advance has been made not in response to any avowed intention to centralize charities generally in the care of the State, but simply because it was essential to give the board this power if its authority in regard to insane already in the State asylums was to be adequate. Nevertheless it has now an important influence on the question of centralization, an influence that will grow with the passage of time.

The private institutions and their administration can give us but slight pause, as they have played but a minor rôle in the charities of the State. On several occasions the State has given its aid, but usually with some reservation whereby it might supervise the expenditure of the sums granted. Its interference has hardly gone any farther than this, however. The most conspicuous instances of State aid are those of a loan of $5,000 to the Orphans' Home at Andrew, made in 1872,[2] to enable it to meet its indebtedness, and the frequent donations to the Benedict Home at Des Moines. The time for payment of the loan to the Orphans' Asylum was extended on several occasions,[3] and finally the State

[1] *L.*, 1900, c. 144.   [2] *L.*, 1872, c. 159.

[3] *L.*, 1882, c. 57 ; 1892, c. 76.

cancelled the debt because of the good done by the institution.[1] The donations to the Benedict Home for Fallen Women have been expended under the direction of the Executive Council, and have been so large that a strong argument has been made for direct participation of the State in its administration.

2. DEVELOPMENT OF THE ADMINISTRATION OF STATE INSTITUTIONS

The first State institution of a charitable, correctional or penal character to develop in Iowa was the penitentiary at Ft. Madison. Its early appearance was due to the grants made in the territorial days by the National Government, and its existence was presupposed in the criminal law of the time which, as now, distinguished felonies from other crimes by the severity of the punishment, all crimes punishable with death, imprisonment at hard labor or in the penitentiary falling in the category of felonies.[2] This institution was of necessity a creation of the State. It was in the grant of State aid to special classes of defectives that the first real step was taken in the assumption by the State of functions of relief that might have developed locally. In 1849 the General Assembly empowered the Auditor, upon certification of the State Superintendent of Public Instruction, to draw his warrant in favor of deaf, dumb and blind applicants for State aid in the sum of fifty dollars for each such applicant.[3] No one beneficiary was allowed more than $100 from the State treasury, and the total amount that might be drawn annually for such purpose was limited to $500 for the education of the deaf and dumb and $250 for the education of the blind.

This system of direct money grants was to endure but a

[1] *L.*, 1892, c. 113.   [2] *L.*, 1838-39, Act Jan. 4.   [3] *L.*, 1849, c. 121.

brief season, however, for soon the institutions for defectives, the insane asylums, the correctional institutions and
the institutions strictly charitable in nature began to make
their appearance. In 1853 provision was made for an Asylum for the Blind to be established at Iowa City, which was
then capital of the State,[1] an institution that was later removed to Vinton. An asylum for the deaf and dumb was
established soon afterwards at Iowa City,[2] later being removed to Council Bluffs. In the Governor's message for
1852 special attention had been called to the need for asylums for the insane. It was stated that there were more
than one hundred pauper insane in the State, one-half of
whom were confined in the common jails, and " thus placed
beyond even a reasonable expectation of recovery," and " the
other moiety * * roaming at large." [3] In response to
this evident need the first insane asylum was established at
Mt. Pleasant in 1855.[4] Gradually the insane population
grew, until now the State has four asylums, the second
asylum being established at Independence in 1868,[5] the third
at Clarinda in 1888,[6] and the fourth, located at Cherokee,
was first provided for in 1892.[7]

The same course of action was followed in the provision
for correctional administration. In 1868 a reform school
for both boys and girls was established.[8] The tendency to
separate the sexes was however soon manifest, and the
several progressions to that end [9] were finally concluded in
1880, when a separate girls' school was established.[10]

In 1872 an additional penitentiary was provided, to be
established " at or near the stone quarries near Anamosa,

[1] *L.*, 1852–53, c. 26.
[3] *Gov. Mess.*, 1852, p. 6.
[5] *L.*, 1868, c. 97.
[7] 1892, c. 80.
[9] See *L.*, 1872, c. 161 ; 1878, c. 105.

[2] *L.*, 1854–55, c. 87.
[4] *L.*, 1854–55, c. 134.
[6] *L.*, 1888, c. 75.
[8] *L.*, 1868, c. 59.
[10] *L.*, 1880, c. 171.

Iowa." [1] In 1876 an institution for the feeble-minded was founded by the State [2] and located at Glenwood. Throughout this period, that is from 1866 on, there were also provisions for industrial homes for the blind,[3] homes for the orphans of soldiers and others,[4] and the soldiers' home.[5]

Several of these institutions received some support from other than State sources, but this did not deter the State from making full provision for their administration and retaining the administration within its own hands.

It will be observed that most of these institutions were established previous to 1870. Up to that time the propriety of their administration by officers or boards individual to each institution was little questioned. There were scathing criticisms, but those that went to the foundation of the system, urging a departure from the independent administration, were few and little regarded. Such changes as were made from 1838 to 1870 were chiefly in the particular administration of the individual institution. Each was viewed as a distinct entity. Each lived its own life, made its own report and settled its own accounts with the State, and the manner of administration and policy pursued by the several institutions were often widely variant in nature. There was no co-operation, and there was not expected to be any. And the lack of co-ordination was not challenged as a fault.

The prevalent type of administration was that by a Board of Trustees having from three to a dozen members, one of whom was generally a resident of the place where the institution was located. These trustees were as a rule chosen by the Legislature, though there were a number of cases in which they were appointed by the Governor independently or with consent of the Council, Census Board or Executive

[1] *L.*, 1872, c. 101.   [2] *L.*, 1876, c. 152.   [3] *L.*, 1870, c. 79; 1890, c. 53.
[4] *L.*, 1866, c. 92; 1868, c. 66; 1876, c. 94.   [5] *L.*, 1886, c. 58; c. 129.

Council. The responsibility for the management of an institution was vested in its own board, which usually had an
extensive rule-making power, authority to appoint its officers and the heads of the institution (who generally appointed
their own subordinates), discharge them, and fix their salaries, within the limits prescribed by law. The chief functions of the trustees were financial in nature. The direct
administration was in most matters left to the executive
head of the institution, be he superintendent, warden or
principal. The trustees ordinarily appointed the financial
officer of the institution. And on his requisitions, when
approved by the superintendent, and sometimes one or more
of the trustees, the funds appropriated by the Legislature
were drawn, such requisitions in the usual case passing to
the Auditor of State to be audited and allowed by him before
a warrant was drawn on the Treasurer of State. A free
hand was often left the boards of trustees in their systems
of accounts. They were little restricted in their manner of
purchasing supplies.[1] And save in the requirement for
reports—which were usually biennial, in a few cases annual
—for regular meetings and for periodical examination of
the accounts and vouchers of institution treasurers, the
boards were not held to many closely defined obligations.

But this is merely the composite of the systems, the common type of administration, as nearly as it may be described.
There were many important exceptions. Particularly was
this true of the penitentiary at Ft. Madison, over which
there was almost unending controversy. Charges of corruption led to committees of investigation; criticism of

---

[1] In 1862, however, a special attempt was made to secure uniformity in the
manner of contracting for and purchasing supplies. *L.*, 1862, c. 46. Similar
efforts appear in subsequent laws, but they were without much success. There
were frequent prohibitions against trustees having interest in institution contracts.
For example, see *L.*, 1878, c. 144.

boards and officers to almost ceaseless experiments in administration.[1]   The penitentiary started with a board of three
directors chosen by the Legislature.   They in turn chose a
superintendent, under whom the construction of the penitentiary was carried on,[2] and also a warden, who held office
at their pleasure.   The system divided responsibility and
was confusing.[3]   Misappropriation of funds and misman-
agement were reputed and proved.   In 1847 the penitentiary was placed under the control of an Agent, answerable
to the General Assembly alone, with no provision for auditing his accounts.[4]   In 1851 a Board of Inspectors and warden appointed by the Governor, with the consent of the Senate, to hold office during the pleasure of the executive, but
not for more than four years under one appointment, were
given charge of the institution.[5]   Again in 1860 there was
a revolutionary change.   This time the warden was made
the sole manager of the institution, under the direction of
the Governor.[6]   But this recital does in no adequate manner reflect the full measure of variety and discontinuity of
the penitentiary's early administration.   A warden chosen
at one time by a superior board,[7] at another by the Governor
and Council or Senate,[8] at another by the General Assembly,[9]
having at one moment only a slight ministerial authority,[10]
at the next thrown into doubt as to whether he had any or

[1] In the issue of the *Iowa Weekly Republican* of February 8, 1860, the editor
said . "These institutions are the bugbear, as they are the fertile theme of endless
discussion . . . The Penitentiary is doubtless in need of appropriations. If the
representations are true concerning it, the *convicts* are simply *tenants at will*.
They are not in so much danger of *breaking* out as *falling* out of their cells."

[2] *L.*, 1838–39, Act Jan. 25.   [3] *L.*, 1840–41, c. 71, well illustrates this.

[4] *L.*, 1846–47, c. 101.   But see *L.*, 1848–49, c. 70.

[5] *Code*, 1851, §§ 3120, 3121.

[6] *L.*, 1860, c. 97.   [7] *L.*, 1856–57, c. 76.   [8] *L.*, 1840–41, c. 71.

[9] *L.*, 1852–53, c. 17.   [10] *L.*, 1838–39, Act Jan. 25.

all power,[1] then raised to assured discretionary authority—
this was the course of one office.[2] The uncertainty per-
vaded every other. There was administration by the Legislature,[3] administration by the Governor,[4] administration
by special boards, administration by the Census Board or
Executive Council,[5] and administration by private lessees.[6]

On the other hand the divergences from the common type
in the administration of the charitable and correctional institutions were not many. Perhaps the most conspicuous
was that in the government of the first insane asylum. It
was provided that a majority of the trustees should reside
in the county where the institution was established.[7] This
was changed later.[8] The Governor, Superintendent of Public Instruction and Secretary were made members of the
first boards of the Blind Asylum [9] and Institution for the
Deaf and Dumb,[10] but within a few years were excluded.
Otherwise the differences were of minor significance.

Such was in general the particular administration of these
institutions to the year 1870, and, in large measure, to 1898.
There were indeed gradually developed some external
checks which, if fully employed, might have secured much

[1] *Compiled Statutes*, 1843, c. 9.   [2] 1860, c. 97.

[3] *L.*, 1845; *Joint Res.*, 13; *L.*, 1845–46, c. 20.

[4] *L.*, 1851, c.[28; 1851, *Joint Res.*, 20; 1872, *Joint Res.*, 23.

[5] *L.*, 1868, c. 104; 1874, c. 35; 1878, c. 110; 1878, c. 186; 1880, c. 149.

[6] *L.*, 1845–46, c. 20. One ill-considered law for leasing the penitentiary provided for no report whatever. The governor commenting upon it said : " In the
absence of information from the proper source, I am only able to state that during
the past year the number of convicts has varied from six to two, the latter being the
number at present in confinement. . . At present there is no discipline whatever,
the convicts are more frequently employed without than within the walls of the
Penitentiary, and can easily make their escape when disposed to do so." *H. J.*;
1846–47, p. 20.

[7] *L.*, 1858, c. 141.   [8] *L.*, 1860, c. 161.

[9] *L.*, 1852–53, c. 26.   [10] *L.*, 1854–55, c. 87.

harmony of policy and some central control. But they
were made little use of.   Passing over the authority of the
Secretary of State, the Governor, or the Executive Council
to approve the official bonds of the officers of the various
institutions, and the detailed duties often required, especially
of the Governor, in the auditing of accounts and checking of
excessive expenditures—powers that, vigorously exercised,
would tend to shape the administration—we may note two
that stand out with unusual prominence.   The first was
the power of the Governor to supervise the penitentiaries.
Monthly reports were to be made to him by the wardens,
and the statute in very careful terms, so hedged about as to
insure if possible their punctilious observance, required the
Governor in person, or through his authorized agent, to
make quarterly investigations of the penitentiaries, and he
was given some minor powers of direct administration.
The Governor perhaps made as full use of this authority
as was compatible with his other duties, certainly a much
greater use than he did of the power early given him to
appoint commissioners of accounts to examine annually the
executive offices of the State and, by intendment, the institutions.[1]   But he did not make such a use that legislative
interference was not often called for, investigating committees necessary, and changes in administration deemed
essential.   The second noteworthy power, or group of
powers, was that bestowed upon the Executive Council, or
Census Board, as it was earlier called.   Given the authority
in 1866 to approve the requisitions of the Orphans' Home,
and in 1868 those of the warden of the penitentiary at Ft.
Madison, its power was gradually extended in several directions.   Contracts for convict labor were usually subject
to its approval.   The few special appropriations for aid to
private charities were expended as it might direct.   In the

provisions for the management of the new State penitentiary at Anamosa the warden was within a few years after
its establishment placed under the direction of the Executive Council in the construction of buildings, purchase of
materials and employment of workmen,[1] and the Council
was given a power, indefinite in terms, but a power for that
very reason capable of a liberal application, to separate prisoners according to age or character.   But these capacities
were little improved, except as they bore upon the financial
conditions.   For the Executive Council was, and has ever
been, loth to consider itself other than a financial or business
board, and has almost never gone beyond its auditing, accounting, examining, assessing and equalizing functions.

The last half of the decade from 1860 to 1870 saw an
increased activity in the affairs of the institutions.   An
unusual number of new institutions was added, and the
public attention was arrested by the spirit of extension.
The expense account commenced to grow until soon it consumed more than half of the appropriations.   And now
began to appear that series of bills which for thirty years
was to seek a reform in the institutional administration,
evoking comment or recommendation in almost every gubernatorial message, all but achieving the reform on more
than one occasion, and finally realizing its object only after
a searching investigation.

It appears that the first bill for State supervision or control was introduced in 1870.[2]   The plan proposed sought
to do away with legislative junketing and provide for State
inspection.   The bill was introduced too late in the session
to be carried.

In 1872 the first step was taken toward central adminis-

[1] *L.*, 1876, c. 137.

[2] *H. F.*, 302, 1870; F. I. Herriott, *Institutional Expenditures in the State
Budgets of Iowa*, p. 73.

tration.   A "Visiting Committee" for the insane asylums
was established.[1]   Its purpose was to protect the insane.
The committee was composed of three members appointed
and removed by the Governor.   They were empowered to
visit the asylums at discretion, though at least one member
must visit the asylums every month.   They were to ascertain " whether any inmates are improperly detained at the
hospital or unjustly placed there, and whether the inmates
are humanely and kindly treated, with full power to correct
any abuses found to exist."   They might discharge any
attendant or employee found guilty of a misdemeanor merit-
ing such discharge.   The measure was resented by many
having to do with the asylums,[2] but it quickly justified its
existence, and though the committee brought to light little
serious abuse, it was well understood that its authority was
a latent safeguard to the interests of the insane, and it remained in high public favor up to the very hour of its super-
session by the Board of Control.   For a short time the
extension of the committee's authority to include that of
a Board of Charities was mooted, the committee with some
diffidence advancing the suggestion [3] and the Governor
heartily seconding it.[4]   The Governor at this time suggested
an advance that has been almost lost sight of since.   He
recommended that the committee should include in the scope
of its duties the examination and suggestion of improvements in the jails and poor houses of the county.   The
advocates of centralization were now in full cry.   In 1876
two bills providing for an Advisory Board were consolidated, and passed the Senate by a strong majority [5] but
failed in the House.

[1] *L.*, 1872, c. 183.   [2] *Gov. Mess.*, 1874, p. 30.
[3] *Report of the Visiting Committee*, 1875, pp. 7, 8.
[4] *Gov. Mess.*, 1876, p. 24.   [5] *S. J.*, 1876, p. 76.

Hardly a session of the Legislature from now on to 1898, when the act creating the Board of Control was passed, ended without its bill for a central board.   In 1878 a bill to create a board of three managers to have charge of all the institutions except the university, the reform schools and the penitentiaries came within the narrowest margin of success.   It had passed the House, a majority of the members of the Senate were in favor of it, and only by the sharpest parliamentary practice was it defeated.   But most of the plans received much less favor.   They varied greatly in nature, some providing for boards with the most meagre advisory capacity, some for boards with authority drawn on even bolder lines than is that of the Board of Control.   Some contained novel features, such as a provision making the board in addition a board of pardons, or a commission in lunacy, or a provision for the extension of supervision over all the State offices as well as the institutions.   One called for central supervision of city and county jails.[1]   The views of the Governors differed quite as radically as did those of legislators.[2]   But the cases were isolated where no form of central supervision was approved.[3]   Almost all interested believed that at least an advisory board for a part of the institutions was called for.   Many would have gone much farther.

At last in 1897 the General Assembly, spurred to definitive action by the persistent rumor of frauds, money misapplied, and favoritism shown in the purchase of supplies

[1] For these various bills see, for 1882, *H. Fs.*, 181, 193; 1884, *H. Fs.*, 128, 307; 1886, *H. Fs.*, 22, 35, 128, 177; 1888, *S. F.*, 68; 1890, *S. Fs.*, 77, 397; 1892, *S. F.*, 18; 1894, *S. F.*, 283.

[2] *Gov. Mess.*, 1878, p. 20; 1880, p. 35; 1882, p. 42; 1884, pp. 37, 43; 1886, pp. 7, 8; 1892, pp. 5, 8; 1894, pp. 5, 7 ; 1896, pp. 4, 5; 1898, pp. 24, 25.   And see in connection, *Governor's Inaugurals*, 1878, p. 14; 1882, pp. 11, 12.

[3] *Gov. Mess.*, 1896, 4, 5, opposed central supervision, except financial examination by the Executive Council.

or in the deposits in banks, appointed a joint committee of the House and Senate to examine thoroughly the several institutions and report on a measure for change in administration. Their report was taken up by the session of 1898, and the result of its action thereon was the present Board of Control. Just previous to this report and the resultant law the Code of 1897 had gone into effect. It contained a provision looking toward more systematic administration that was somewhat lost to view in the interest attending the new law. Under the code the Executive Council were to devise a system of book-keeping or accounts for all the State institutions, and to make annual expert examinations of their accounts and financial transactions.[1] These powers, as well as those of the Governor with respect to the penitentiaries, were transferred to the Board of Control.

The report of the Healy Investigating Committee of 1897 is the one document of prime importance in the history of the State charities and corrections. It constitutes a cogent and severe arraignment of institutional administrative independence. Faults and blemishes it found on almost every hand. Lack of uniform method in the purchasing of supplies for subsistence or construction purposes; the consumption of different grades of supplies in hospitals treating the same kind of patients; the intermingling of different funds in violation of law; the non-observance of statutory limitations in expenditures for specific purposes; total failure in some places to audit bills, or auditing after the bills were paid; the payment of different salaries for the same services by institutions of the same character;[2] these were among its general criticisms. In some cases the report showed that though the law required orders on the treasurer of an institution to be signed by the president and secretary, the president had been accustomed to sign such orders in blank

[1] *Code*, 1897, §§ 158–163.   [2] *Healy Report*, p. 67.

and leave them with the secretary to be filled out and signed
by him when the occasion required.[1]   It advised the Legislature that notwithstanding express prohibitions appropriations were very generally disbursed from the State treasury
weeks and months before actually needed and deposited in
local banks, that an institution was very generally considered the lawful prey of the locality in which it was situated,
and the bulk of the supplies bought from local merchants.[2]
It noted a feeling of hostility between institutions and a
feeling of opposition toward them on the part of public
and Legislature, induced by the sentiment that institutions
were the vehicles of special interests, and not unselfishly
representative of a beneficent purpose of government.[3]   The
facts were incontrovertible.   The demand for reform was
imperative.   This the investigating committee appreciated
fully, and it said, " If we thought the Legislature competent to remedy the defects, abuses and evils presented in
our report, by enactments applicable to each institution,
there would be much merit in suggesting specific changes.
Entertaining the opinion, however, that the major part of
our criticisms refer to abuses inhering in the trustee system, a thorough measure of reform is the only remedy.
We attempted with some care to prepare a list of statutory
amendments, but on reflection it was ascertained that the
greater number of such amendments can properly form a
part of a measure creating a central or supervisory board.
Many other of such amendments will not be required if
such board is established.   The disease is organic, and too
deep-seated for the use of palliatives." [4]

But the step to the new order was not unattended by the
controversy that has marked the advance with weariful
slowness in other States.   In fact the dispute of thirty years

[1] *Healy Report*, pp. 61, 62.   [2] *Ibid.*, pp. 14, 29.
[3] *Ibid.*, p. 66.   [4] *Ibid.*, p. 65.

was revamped. All that had been said before, pro or con, was repeated here again. By conferring upon the board executive power, it was said that its function as an advisory board would be impaired " in the same sense and to the same extent as an attorney would be injured in his professional career by requiring him to perform the work of a book-keeper." How could a board inspect and supervise itself? For it was declared with much apparent force that the managers of an institution are, in the eye of the law, the institution, and that many of the advantages of a State board, as such a board is commonly understood, are therefore lost if there is no intermediate authority between the managers and the legislators, the Governor and the people. The point of remuneration was dwelt upon at length. Under the Code of 1897 the members of most boards of trustees had been allowed four dollars *per diem* and traveling expenses, but they could not receive compensation for more than thirty days in each year. Those opposing the central salaried board contended that once a price was attached the office immediately became a prize, of political seductiveness. Three thousand dollars is a good wage for a decayed politician. And price and payment would keep out that class of men, an able class, willing to give their services to the charitable work of the State, but unwilling to have them estimated at a pittance. To this and like opposition, and to the claim that the power of the board should be a moral power solely, perhaps the strongest argument of those who favored the Board of Control was that of economy and business expediency and efficiency, in short of scientific adjustment.

It is acknowledged by those who oppose the doctrine or practice of gratuitous service that perhaps it occupies a stronghold when used in benevolent or semi-benevolent institutions. Hence it was with some difficulty that the

salaried office could be made to win support, but that was
accomplished, and again by means of the argument of
its superiority from a business point of view. The arguments that the motives that lead men to give their service without pay are not constant, therefore not reliable,
that the public servant, serving without compensation, cannot be held to strict accountability, that gratuitous service
is never a trained service,[1] were brought into play and
victory was won for the Board of Control. The thought
of the legislators of Iowa when they brought this strong
and virile innovation into the administration of the institutions of the State was the thought of Walter Bagehot
when he wrote: "A very high pay of prestige is almost
always very dangerous. It causes the post to be desired
by vain men, by lazy men, by men of rank, and when that
post is one of real and technical business, and when therefore it requires much previous training, much continuous
labor, and much patient and quick judgment, all such men
are dangerous." [2] The members of the Board of Control
qualified April 6, 1898, not assuming control of the institutions, however, until July 1, 1898.

II THE PRESENT ADMINISTRATION—THE BOARD OF CONTROL

The Board of Control of State Institutions is composed
of three electors of the State, appointed by the Governor,
with the consent of two-thirds of the Senate. Not more
than two of the members may be of the same political
party, and no two may reside at the time of their appointment in the same congressional district. The nominations
of the Governor may not be considered by the Senate until
referred to a committee of five, not more than three of

[1] *Cf.* H. C. Adams, *Science of Finance*, pp. 16, 18.
Lombard Street, p. 225.

whom may be of the same political party. The term of
the office is, regularly, six years, but in order that the offices
of all three members might not be terminable at the same
time it was provided in the statute creating the board that
the appointments, in the first instance, should be for two,
four and six years respectively.

The power of removal was placed in the hands of the
Governor and the Senate, the Governor being authorized,
with the consent of the Senate, during a session of the
General Assembly, to remove any member of the board for
malfeasance or nonfeasance in office, or for any cause that
would render him ineligible to appointment or incapable
or unfit to discharge the duties of his office. A removal
so made is final. When the Assembly is not in session the
Governor may suspend any member so disqualified and appoint another to fill the vacancy, subject, however, to the
action of the Senate when next in session.

The salary of the members of the board is $3,000 per
annum. Each member is required to take an oath and give
an official bond in the sum of $25,000, signed by sureties
approved by the Governor. It is provided, by way of
eliminating the political and corruptive tendencies of public
office, that no member of the board may be eligible to any
other lucrative office in the State during his term of service,
or for one year thereafter, or to any position in any State
institution during the term for which he was appointed,
nor within one year after the expiration of his term. A
precaution looking to similar ends is taken in the section
relative to the prohibition of political influence or contribution. It is provided that any member or officer of the
board or any officer or employee of a State institution subject to the board who, by solicitation or otherwise, exerts
his influence, directly or indirectly, to induce other officers
or employees of the State to adopt his political views or to

favor any particular person or candidate for office, or who in any manner contributes money or other thing of value to any person for election purposes, shall be removed from his office or position by the proper authorities.[1] Two years after the creation of the board a further law was framed, on the recommendation of its members, to entrench the board yet more firmly in its independence. It was provided then that the levying of political assessments upon employees of the board should be prohibited, and it was made a misdemeanor to demand or solicit from any officer or employee of any institution under the control of the board a contribution for election purposes, or for the payment of the expenses of any political committee or organization. The significance of this law is shown by the general report, that in 1901 the State central committee of the party in power levied a tax of four per cent. on the wages of all State house employees. In 1902 the tax was three per cent.[2] The integrity of the members is further assured by the provision that it shall be a crime for any one of them to accept a gift from a person or firm dealing with the institutions under its charge.

The chairman of the board for each biennial period is that member whose term of office expires first. The board is authorized to employ a secretary at a salary of two thousand dollars per annum, a stenographer, and such other assistants as it may need. It has an official seal, attesting therewith all commissions, orders or other papers issued by it. An itemized statement of the expenses of the board and its employees, properly certified, must be presented to the Governor for his written audit before payment is made. The salaries and expenses of the board are paid monthly by the Treasurer of State upon the warrant of the Auditor.

[1] *L.*, 1898, c. 118, § 35.

[2] *The Register and Leader*, of Des Moines, Ia., Sept. 7, 1902.

Turning now more specifically to the relation of the board to the Legislature, the following matters arrest our attention: The board is required to prepare biennial estimates of the appropriations necessary to be made for the support of the several institutions, and for the extraordinary and special expenditures for buildings, betterments or other improvements. Suggestions for the benefit of the several institutions or for the dependent, defective or criminal classes of the State are to be included in such reports. And, on request, the board or its committee must attend meetings of the legislative committees, to which such questions may be submitted, and furnish information that may be demanded. The board is also subject to the examination of the joint legislative committee on retrenchment and reform. It owes a duty of reporting to the Governor. Any wrong or abuse alleged to exist in the State institutions under its control it is required to investigate and report to him.

It would require many pages to set forth in comprehensive detail the varied relations and powers of the board. The purpose of this study will be as successfully served if they are noted in broad capitulation. With respect to the branches of the administration under its supervision the powers of the board are three-fold. First, it has the general control, including policy, finance and every element of administration, of the State charitable, penal and reformatory institutions. Second, it exercises a financial surveillance over the affairs of the State institutions of advanced or higher education. In the third place, subsequent to its creation, it was given the authority mentioned in the historical outline to inspect, and indeed administer to a large degree, county or private institutions in which the insane are kept. The powers over the educational institutions and the local institutions for the insane are incidental and sup-

plementary. As the *raison d'etre* of the board was the
unsatisfactory administration of the State charities and corrections, its chief functions of a necessity have to do with
them.

The institutions under the control of the board are the
four State hospitals for the insane, the college for the blind,
the school for the deaf, the institution for the feeble-minded,
the soldiers' home, the industrial school for boys, the industrial school for girls, the industrial reformatory for females [1]
and the two State penitentiaries.

The key to the strength of any administrative officer
or body is his or its authority over subordinates. Such
authority is the imperative condition of effective control.
And here there is nothing wanting in the power of the
board, for while the executive head of each of the above
institutions has the power to appoint and remove subordinates, the executive head himself is appointed and removed
by the board. To make the board responsible for the whole,
but at the same time to make the obligations and powers of
each executive chief stand out in bold outline in his particular sphere, these are the principles of this system. And
so far has this purpose to centralize authority, first in the
board, secondly in the heads of the various institutions, been
carried that it is made a misdemeanor for any member of
the board to suggest the appointment of any person under
a chief executive officer. "Thus we have in effect civil
service," remarks a member, "for every subordinate officer
and employee of the institution knows that he holds his
place at the will of the chief executive of such institution.
Attention to duty, ability and efficiency in service are the
only tests. No appointments are influenced by any political
considerations whatever.[2]

[1] Created by *L.*, 1900, c. 102.
[2] *Conference of Charities and Corrections*, 1900, p. 173.

The powers of direct administration possessed by the board with respect to these institutions are in general perhaps even larger than might be expected in a central correlating and directing authority. The board has power to investigate the management and financial condition of the institutions. It inquires into questions of insanity of patients, determines when insane persons may be admitted at the charge of the State, and divides the State into penitentiary and hospital districts. It compels the providing of fire protection and fire escapes. It takes pains that all employees handling money or property of the State shall give bond. It is empowered to require certain officers to take inventories annually of all the State's movable property, and quarterly of all supplies and stores, and it annually fixes the salaries of all officers and employees of the institutions except the chief executive officers. It has power to investigate the question of insanity and condition of any person committed to any State hospital, and may discharge any person so committed, on securing the recommendation of the superintendent of the institution. The board may transfer patients or convicts from one institution to another. It has power to arrange for the care or transportation of insane patients whose residences are unknown, and in cases of questionable commitment may investigate. And in 1900 the board was given power to direct the purchase of materials or any articles of supply by one institution from another, the value to be fixed by the board at the reasonable market price, and the payments therefor as between institutions to be made in the manner provided for the payments for supplies. Two of the most prominent powers of direct administration are those existing in connection with the board's duty to provide a system of financial accounts and book-keeping, and its authority to purchase supplies for the State institutions. Sporadic attempts had been made to

accomplish both of these administrative betterments in some
measure previous to the creation of the Board of Control,
but not until its creation was success attained.

The scheme of book-keeping, of accounts and of the purchase of and payment for supplies as adopted in pursuance
of the mandate of the statute is, at first blush, complicated.
And yet it is in reality simple, so far as control necessarily
involving many progressions and checks can be simple.
Each step has the virtue of clear demarcation. Conflict,
overlapping, with the attendant dangers of shifted responsibility and misplaced censure, are wholly eliminated.

We may note in some detail the methods used in the
purchase of supplies, for they illustrate very clearly the
pains that have been taken not only on this but on every
hand to secure expert administration. The aim of the system is to secure lower prices through purchase of gross
quantities and through competitive bids. Once a year the
superintendent of each institution is required to make estimates, in duplicate, for coal, flour and canned goods; once
every three months for all other supplies. These estimates
are forwarded to the office of the board, there to be subjected first to the scrutiny of the estimate clerk. Errors in
computation, classification, footings—all these he corrects.
To each estimate he then attaches a memorandum of his
alterations, and makes note of matter proper for the board's
consideration. Now the estimates are passed upon by the
board, reduced or increased, or in any way changed as to
estimated prices. The board having approved the corrected
papers, one copy is returned to the institution and one filed
in the office of the board. Considerable margin is allowed
for changes at this, the plastic, stage of these little quasi-bud-
gets of the institutions. Estimates noticeably defective as to
substance, or defective in the important formal requirements
of signature and certification, are speedily returned for cor-

rection. And supplemental estimates and re-estimates are
allowed where conditions suggest their value.

A trick has been appropriated from the ingenious device
of card catalogues in the choice of colored inks for estimates.
These inks differ according to the funds out of which the
estimates are to be paid, blanks for articles to be paid for
out of the support fund being printed in black ink, those to
be paid for out of special appropriations in red ink, and so on.

The next step is the making up of the schedules. After
the 10th of January, April, July and October, when all the
estimates are in the hands of the board, separate schedules
of all articles estimated for are made up for each institution.
The schedules are sent with printed specifications to all bid-
ders and wholesale dealers in the goods required in Iowa,
and to many in the large cities of neighboring States. Samples must accompany the bids in many instances. When
the bids and samples are ready the quarterly meeting of the
superintendents of the institutions is held. The superintendents inspect bids and samples, leaving a written note
with the board indicating their preference. The board
then, with the assistance of a single superintendent, makes
the awards. Then follow the shipping and checking in,
both conducted according to carefully prescribed and enforced rules of procedure. And when the goods are checked
in the stewards make duplicate vouchers therefor, which are
sent to the sellers for their verification.

Next in order is the payment of the bills. In this process
vouchers for supplies pass through the same mill as the
other vouchers and the pay rolls. The pay roll and all
vouchers are certified to the board at the end of each month,
and are immediately placed in the hands of the estimate
clerk. He compares the pay roll with the schedule of salaries and indicates the errors therein, and he examines and
makes memoranda as to the addition and computation in

the vouchers. They then come before the board for action, accompanied by a memorandum in red ink, showing the balances in the several funds, out of which these vouchers must be paid, the object being to keep ever before the board the fact as to whether they have balances to the credit of the institutions in those particular funds. The examination that follows by the board is carefully made, and it is the practice for it to return the pay roll or any voucher for correction, and whenever a successful bidder has failed to furnish the article contracted for, or has furnished an inferior article, it directs the superintendent of the institution concerned to return the goods or to make a proper rebate on the voucher. Upon approval of the pay roll and vouchers by the board the secretary makes triplicate certificates, one to be sent to the State Auditor, one to the State Treasurer, and one to be retained in the office of the board. All bills are certified in the names of the parties to whom they are due, and on receipt of these certificates and warrant from the State Auditor, the State Treasurer mails a check to each of such certified persons. On the other hand the full amount of the pay roll in each case is certified to be paid to the superintendent, who disburses it to the several employees.

A recent chairman of the board in reviewing this procedure observes with emphasis that the system is such that the board does not handle a dollar, and that the superintendent of each institution handles no money except the pay roll, which he receives for disbursement among the employees, and what may be derived from the sales of the product of farms or institution shops, which must be reported monthly and sent in to the State Treasurer. The system has met with the degree of success that leads him to assert: "After very many examinations in different States of the system of book-keeping and purchasing supplies, I have found none where they are in all respects like that we

pursue in our own State, and none equal to our system."
The system has remained unaltered.[1]

Emphasis is laid by the law upon careful statistical reports, as upon technique throughout.   The board is called
upon to furnish each institution with books and blanks for
statistical records and returns.   Duplicates are kept in the
office of the board, upon which entries are made when the
returns come in.   Provisions conducing to the dissemination of information and an enlightened policy are prominent
features of the law.   It is provided that the board shall
gather and present information embodying the experience
of soldiers' homes, charitable, reformatory and penal institutions in this and other countries, also regarding the most
successful methods of caring for the insane, delinquent and
criminal classes.   And the duty is enjoined upon it of encouraging scientific investigation of the treatment of epi-
lepsy by the medical staff of the insane hospitals and the
institution for the feeble-minded.   It is required to publish
from time to time bulletins and reports of the scientific and
clinical work in such institutions.   The publication issued
by the board quarterly, called *The Bulletin,* bespeaks the
great activity in the educational work of the board.   In it,
besides leading articles, usually scientific papers read before
the quarterly conferences of the superintendents of the several institutions with the board, are published the reports
of the meetings of these conferences.   These quarterly meetings are prescribed by the law.   They have been the source
of much benefit.   Even a superficial examination of the
reports of the meetings will reveal the alertness of the superintendents, the genuine interest of those participating, and
how nearly these conferences have approached the true par-
liament of administrative education.   This work is all sup-
plemented by the visitatorial power and duty of the board.

[1] *Report of the Board of Control,* 1901, p. 7.

It must visit all institutions once every six months, and the hospitals must be visited by one of its own members or its secretary every month.   In fact the visits actually made are more numerous than the law demands.   Frequently all three members of the board make the visits required.   The visits usually cover two days, sometimes more.[1]

The supervision by the board of the financial affairs of the State institutions of advanced or higher education is scarcely of a piece with the general intent of its existence. It is required to investigate thoroughly the reports and transactions of regents of the State University, the trustees of the State Normal School, and the trustees of the State College of Agriculture and Mechanic Arts, and the books and records of such institutions, for the purpose of ascertaining:

" 1. Whether the persons holding positions have faithfully accounted for all moneys of the State which have been drawn from the State treasury or have come into their hands or otherwise.

" 2. If appropriations have been drawn from the State treasury in accordance with the law and so expended.

" 3. Whether such persons have drawn money for services, *per diem,* mileage, or expenses, or otherwise, not authorized by law, or have authorized expenditures without authority of law."

The third branch of the board's authority is the most instructive, instructive because it comes as a second thought in this system of administration, and because it indicates the line of evolution.   It seems to declare that the concomitant of centralized administration of the State institutions is to be the central control of local institutions of generic type.   At every session of the Legislature since the creation of the board a step has been taken in this direction,

[1] *Report of the Board of Control,* 1901, pp. 113-115.

the most recent of this class of powers, that of inspecting and supervising societies for the care of friendless children, having been added in 1902. The power to supervise the county and private institutions in which insane persons are kept has many elements of strength.

The board is required to visit and inspect all such institutions at least twice annually by one or more of its members or by its duly appointed representative. The first inspections were made by members of the board personally in order that they might know of the conditions prevailing in these institutions, and so judge of the merits of the reports of subsequent inspections. Superintendents and assistant physicians of the insane hospitals were also appointed to make these inspections.

The board has power to make rules and regulations touching the care and treatment of insane in such institutions. The rules adopted have been aimed to safeguard their treatment; they have required the establishment of night watches at institutions when necessary, the proper number of attendants, fire escapes, medical aid and so forth. In case any institution fails to comply with these rules the board is authorized to remove all insane persons kept therein at public expense to some other institution, State, county or private, at the expense of the county which sent the patient to the institution in question. But the board also has a discretionary power of removal even in case of compliance with the rules. There have been very few cases of noncompliance, still the removals have been numerous. During the first year in which the law was in operation forty-seven patients were removed from county and private institutions to State hospitals, and seventy-two from State hospitals to county and private institutions.[1] Complementary to this power is the authority possessed by the board when it be-

[1] *Report of the Board of Control,* 1901, p. 55.

lieves any person in any such institution sane or illegally re-
strained of liberty to institute proceedings for his discharge.

The question now naturally arises, what have been the
successes of this rather ambitious plan of reform? The
answer must be that, on the whole, they have been remarkable. They are the most obvious in the financial results.
The Legislature had reduced the expense of the support of
the inmates in the aggregate by $100,000 before the board
took charge of the institutions, and yet in the first year of
operation, of the support funds allowed over $119,000 re-
mained unexpended. And it appears that notwithstanding
this there were many improvements in new machinery, that
the food and clothing were better than they had been under
the old system. It is said, too, that the personnel of the
employees was improved, but there have not been wanting
some assertions that this is a mistaken statement, that for
a brief time the board took a step backward in this respect,
the result of too ambitious reforms.

The State Treasurer in his report for 1899 computed
the decrease in cost of operating the institutions under the
control of the board for the first year, as compared with
the previous year, at $379,490.73, or 26.9 per cent.[1] The
expenses from the support fund for the biennial period
ending June 30th, 1901, were but little more than those for
the period ending June 30, 1899,[2] thus giving an earnest
of continued economy. A comparison of the expenditures
for the Iowa institutions with those for other States under
the decentralized methods of management is also favorable
to the Iowa plan.[3]

[1] *Treasurer's Report*, 1899, p. lxii.

[2] In the period 1897–1899, they were $2,114,619.75 ; 1899–1901, they were
$2,167,906.07.

[3] For the year ending June 30, 1899, the per capita expenditures for the Iowa
institutions were $145.50 as against $175.68 in New York; $183.00 in Minne-

The other results are less capable of statistical demonstration. The service resulting has been declared by some better than that of any State having a formal civil service commission. The care of the inmates, and especially of the insane, has improved. The creation of the office of State architect has been a great benefit. This officer receives the same salary as the members of the board, and gives all his time to the preparation of plans for additions to or improvements in the institutions and the supervision of the execution of such plans. A most conspicuous result is seen in the steps taken toward the improvement of local institutions where the insane are kept.[1] The board's investigations revealed that in them troublesome inmates were locked up and treated as criminals, and that the food and wearing apparel was in many cases very poor. It was shown that little or no attention had been paid to the cleanliness and personal habits of the inmates. In some institutions as many as six or more inmates were bathed in the same water; in some they were seldom or never bathed. In numerous cases the rooms in which inmates were kept and the furniture were filthy beyond description, walls and ceilings broken, and vermin found in furniture, beds, floors, walls and ceilings. There were cases where men had unobstructed access to the rooms of insane women. These bad conditions were largely the result of the policy of awarding contracts for keeping the poor and insane to the lowest bidder, or to persons with ability to care for poor farms without regard to their qualifications for caring for the insane. The board

---

sota, and $187.40 in Michigan for the years ending respectively June 30, July 31 and September 30, all in the year 1900. Moreover, the variation in the per capita cost of different institutions was much wider in these States than in Iowa under the Board of Control.

[1] One of the most striking results is seen in the greater reliability of the information secured under the centralized system. For example, see *Report of Board of Control*, 1901, p. 57.

has closed those institutions which were not taking reasonably good care of the insane, and has greatly improved the condition and management of others. It has discouraged the counties from attempting to care for a small number of insane, though according to the late reports there are still thirty-one counties caring for insane fewer in number than twelve, and in nearly all these counties the insane are kept with and treated the same as the poor, though the law provides for separate care and different treatment.

And lastly the high personnel of the Board of Control is to be noted. The charitable and correctional interests of the State have drawn to their service men most highly esteemed in the community and State of which they are citizens, men qualified to see eye to eye and to maintain a safe equilibrium between the social and financial demands of their charge. Thus the contention that such a system would draw to its service the mere political camp follower has been confuted. Indeed, one cannot examine the work of this board without profound admiration for its singleness of vision, its unqualified aim to do the greatest good both for the individual inmate and the general State interest. Seldom or never has an official department of the State of Iowa found it so easy to secure from the Legislature the laws that it recommends or the appropriations that it asks. This is the best evidence of the general satisfaction with the system and the thorough confidence in those to whose care it has been confided. This implicit faith has been such indeed that it has induced legislation which in the future may in less worthy hands, should the board ever know such, prove very dangerous. In its first report the board asked that it be given authority to expend unused balances for any purpose deemed necessary for the several institutions.[1] This

---

[1] *Report of the Board of Control*, 1899, p. 52.

authority was granted.[1]   It means that the unrestricted control of the balances has been transferred from legislative to
administrative hands.   And it must be admitted that this
is a rather startling departure from the principle of democratic control of public expenditures.[2]

To the inquiry as to the future of the administration of
charities and corrections it may be said that centralization
might be rationally extended in two directions.   Indeed,
such extensions may prove imperative.   In the first place
the care of the unfortunate or delinquent may be made less
a local and more a State charge.   This is especially urged
with respect to the care of the insane.   The Board of Control has recommended that the support of this class be
entirely taken over by the State.[3]   The other direction,
and perhaps the more important one, is that of the central
supervision of city and county jails and the local poor relief.
It is remarkable how little discussion there has been of this
question in the history of Iowa.   The jails have been left
under the wing of the district courts and the local judicial
functionaries in a very haphazard way, and no one has asked
whether the inspections have been made as required or wor-
ried himself about the care of prisoners.   And yet it is
doubtless true that an investigation would reveal conditions
similar to those shown by the Board of Control to have
existed in the local institutions where the insane are kept,
and, incidentally, in the poor houses generally.   The county
care of dependents has been discussed, but as yet little or
nothing has been done to better it.[4]   All that the Board of
Control has shown with respect to the county care of the

[1] *L.*, 1900, c. 150.

[2] *Cf.* Herriott, *op. cit.*, p. 55.

[3] *Report of Board of Control*, 1901, p. 51.

[4] See W. R. Patterson, *County Care of Dependents in Iowa*, in *Bulletin of
Iowa State Institutions*, vol. iii, no. 4, p. 518.

insane may be repeated with respect to county care of the poor. In addition there are to be found among others such evils as the mingling of insane and defectives with the poor, of children in arms or of tender years with adults, the greatest disparity in systems of book-keeping, the elevation of graduates of the road supervisorship through mere political " pull " to the position of poor-master, and small salaries and inefficient service. The Board of Control has not recommended that it be given power to supervise the poor houses or jails. It is probable that its present great power makes it diffident about asking further authority. It would indeed be a mistake to give the board such power without at the same time making a very liberal appropriation and adding largely to its force of inspectors. Already it has declared its inability, because of other duties, to make further personal inspection of the local institutions where the insane are kept, and this work is now done by its agents. It has been recommended that a State board of charities be created, having supervision of the county care of dependents,[1] and there would be some advantages in a distinct board having such powers, and perhaps having powers to inspect the jails. But inasmuch as the experience of the Board of Control must prove of immeasurable advantage in such a service, there seems a stronger argument for adding to the membership of the board and its assistants as may be necessary, and making it the one central administrative authority in all these matters.

[1] Patterson, *loc. cit.*, p. 527.

CHAPTER IV

PUBLIC HEALTH AND SAFETY

I HISTORICAL SKETCH OF THE ADMINISTRATION OF PUBLIC HEALTH AND SAFETY

ONLY within recent years has the health administration been considered in Iowa as much more than an accidental phase of government. The death rate of Iowa has usually been low. An inland State, it has been free from those epidemics of foreign importation which occasionally have ravaged the coast States, epidemics that have caused the insistence upon strict quarantine and preventive measures. The advancement of the health administration in a number of the Eastern States has often been given its primary impetus by the yellow fever, the Asiatic cholera or other scourge from abroad, until the State afflicted has made a virtue of necessity and brought its health administration to a high degree of perfection. There has been no such spur to the Iowa law-makers. Moreover, the lack of large cities and the diffusion of the population over extensive areas have tended to conceal or moderate the appearances of disease even when of serious extent, disease that might in congested districts, because of its more evident destruction, have awakened public clamor for reform. Add to this the general conviction, founded as it is in fact, that the health of the State is unusually good, and it needs little further to explain the slowness with which the machinery of health administration has developed.

From the years of its territorial existence until 1866 the health administration of Iowa was purely an incidental function. Little stress was laid upon it in the laws; less attention given to it in practice. The evidence is slight, but it can be readily deduced that the conditions during this period were indeed salubrious. Quite as naturally as preambles appear before constitutions, or enacting clauses before the substance of laws, did the formula of congratulation upon the good health of the State appear as the opening sentence in the Governor's message of this time. " Since the termination of the last meeting of the Legislative Assembly, it has pleased the Almighty Power, in whose hands we are, to vouchsafe to the people of this territory as great a degree of exemption from disease as has fallen to the lot of any portion of our extensive country," [1] thus began almost every message of the territorial and the early State period. There are one or two references to disease,[2] but never indications that such disease had taken on calamitous proportions. The advertisements of immigration agencies of the time, and the pamphlets prepared by various communities to induce settlement, painted in glowing colors the great healthfulness of the climate. Though the utterances of interested parties, they seem to have been not without a considerable basis in truth. It was not against natural causes of death that the pioneer sought to protect himself by legislative enactment. He would leave that to Providence and his own good care. The frontier desperado, the Indian and the wolf, these were the subjects of his particular solicitude and his measures for safety.[3] Public sanitation would have seemed a pretty and useless plaything in such circumstances, and he gave it almost no thought.

[1] *Gov. Mess.*, Dec. 6, 1843.

[2] *Gov. Mess.*, 1850, *H. J.*, 1850-51, p. 8.

[3] See *L.*, 1839-40, c. 27.

Nowhere is the incidental character of the health administration better illustrated than in the charters of the early towns and cities. On January 23, 1839, " the President and Trustees of the Town of Bloomington " were incorporated, the first municipal charter under the separate territorial organization.[1] The subject of health was not mentioned in it, the nearest approach thereto being the power granted *the electors* to remove nuisances or provide for their removal. Two days afterward, however, Davenport was incorporated,[2] with somewhat different and wider powers. In this case the Mayor, recorder and trustees, or a majority of them, were given power to make by-laws and ordinances " for the promotion of morality, as well as for the good regulation, interest, safety, health, cleanliness and conveniences of said town and the citizens thereof." And it was further provided that " the said corporation shall have power to regulate and improve all streets, alleys, sidewalks, drains or sewers, to sink and keep in repair public wells, remove nuisances."

Substantially all of the charters from now on to 1850 followed the one form or the other, either giving the electors of the city a general power to abate or provide for the abatement of nuisances,[3] or lodging a power, general or specific, with the city officers and trustees.[4] In both cases, however, the function was patently incidental and little emphasized. By 1850 the first form was practically abandoned, and from then on the powers were placed in the

[1] *L.*, 1838–39, Jan. 23.   [2] *Ibid.*, Jan. 25.

[3] For charters illustrative, see Farmington, *L.*, 1840–41, c. 44 ; Iowa City, *L.*, 1840–41, c. 39 ; Mt. Pleasant, *L.*, 1841–42, c. 19.

[4] For charters illustrative, see Ft. Madison, *L.*, 1841–42, c. 89 ; Keosauqua, *L.*, 1841–42, c. 122 ; Farmington, *L.*, 1846–47, c. 79 ; Fairfield, *L.*, 1846–47, c. 38. The charter of Burlington, *L.*, 1845, c. 54, went into unusual detail in respect to the health administration ; same in Dubuque, *L.*, 1845–46, c. 123.

hands of the city councils. In the session of the General Assembly of 1850-51 some thirteen towns and cities were granted charters, and in no instance were the powers in question confided to the electors.

The first provision for the self-incorporation of towns and cities was made by the Code of 1851, and this also followed the second form. It provided that the charters of self-incorporation might give power to establish such ordinances as were necessary for good regulation, safety, health and cleanliness, to provide for drains, sewers, public wells, wharves and landing places, and " to make any other ordinary, suitable and proper police regulations." [1]

The laws begin to place a little further emphasis upon the health administration in 1853, but it is still treated as ·of secondary importance. About this time we find special provision for health officers, indicating that it is now becoming a distinctive function. At this time Council Bluffs was granted a charter,[2] in which the council was empowered to appoint, in such manner as it should determine, street commissioners, a clerk of the market, health officers and such other officers as it might deem advisable. It was also given authority to prescribe their duties, their powers and qualifications, and might provide for the election of any such officers by the citizens. But these provisions were not of great significance, for a number of charters were subsequently allowed containing no such provisions.[3]

The Constitution of 1857 put an end to the special incorporation of cities and towns.[4] It provided they should in all cases be incorporated under general laws. In pursuance of this the Legislature in 1858 passed a law pro-

[1] *Code*, 1851, § 665.   [2] *L.*, 1851–53, c. 64.
[3] Notably that of Des Moines, *L.*, 1856–57, c. 185.
[4] *Cons.*, 1857, Art. 4, § 30.

viding for general incorporation, by which cities were to be divided into two classes, according to population.[1] All places having a population of 15,000 or over were to be deemed cities of the first class, all having a population of 2,000 were cities of the second class, while the remaining incorporations were to be known as incorporated towns. And the law provided that councils of cities, but not towns, should have power to establish boards of health, with powers sufficient to secure the inhabitants of the city " from the evils, distresses and calamities of contagious, malignant and infectious diseases." Here is found for the first time the provision for a board of health and direct consideration of contagious diseases, but it is to be noted that the law is permissive merely, and that there is no enforceable obligation resting upon the city council to provide for such a board.

It was not until 1866 that the health administration was made a specific and certain, because an obligatory, function. In that year an act was passed constituting the Mayor and council of any incorporated town or city, or the trustees of any township not incorporated, a board of health.[2] The powers of such local boards were full, definite and described in considerable detail. They were given power to make rules and regulations respecting nuisances, sources of filth and causes of sickness, to remove and abate them, and to publish these regulations. More specifically, they might make regulations concerning the cleansing of streets, alleys and drains, concerning the communication with houses where there was any infectious or contagious disease. They might establish pest houses and hospitals and remove patients thereto. To carry out their work they were authorized to employ all assistants necessary, fix their compensation, and employ physicians in cases of poverty. They were empowered to levy a tax for the expenses so incurred, and

[1] *L.*, 1858, c. 157.   [2] *L.*, 1866, c. 107.

the sanction of their action was found in the provision that wilful violation of their regulations should be a misdemeanor, subject to fine or imprisonment.

Later laws have not much altered these provisions. In 1880 it was enacted that every local board of health should appoint a competent physician to the board, who should be the health officer of the city, town or village, such officer to hold his place at the pleasure of the board.[1] In 1882 cities under special charters, which hitherto had been neglected in the general health laws, received legislative attention, and a board of health somewhat different from that of the general incorporations was established.[2] It was provided that the Mayor and aldermen of each city under special charter should have full power to appoint a local board of health consisting of three or five members, but it was stipulated that a majority should be members of the city council, and that the Mayor should be a member and chairman *ex officio*. The powers of boards so constituted were, if anything, wider than those under the general law. For example, the board was given power, with consent of the city council, to prohibit by public proclamation the congregation of people in schools, churches and other public places in case of small-pox and other infectious diseases, also to forbid unvaccinated persons attending public assemblages.

The results of the establishment of local boards of health were not particularly obvious. In many cases things seemed to go much as they had before, in many the law was not observed. There was no general outbreak of disease, no impending disasters to quicken the popular interest, inspire the popular demand and so read the law into the life of the local administration. Things crept in the health administration. And it was not in wide-awake response to an

[1] *L.*, 1882, c. 168.   [2] *L.*, 1882, c. 168.

insistent summons that the next great step was taken, but, as before, sleepily and carelessly that it came about.

This next supreme move was the creation of the State Board of Health. The law for its establishment was passed in 1880.[1] Governor John H. Gear in his inaugural address of January 17, 1878, had made the first official mention of its possible establishment, but his recommendation did not call for a board of health as the institution is at present understood. He said that he had been requested repeatedly by the medical profession of the State to call the attention of the General Assembly to the necessity of establishing a State Board of Health, " whose duty it should be to pass upon the qualifications of practicing physicians, in order that the people may be protected from empiricism." But here his recommendation ended. His biennial message of 1880, however, pushed the matter a step farther. He now advised that the board should be created with the further powers of adopting measures for the protection of the health of the people generally and for the collection of vital statistics of the State. The suggestion, so extended, met with the favor of the Legislature, and this year the State Board of Health was created.

The powers thus conferred upon the nine appointive, unsalaried members who composed the State board were taken up with ardor and the expectation of great benefits to the State. The final reason for the creation of the board seemed to have been that of securing vital statistics, and it was on this feature that the greatest emphasis was laid in the first few years. Indeed, the second biennial report of the board, made in 1883, was the most voluminous report that had been attempted up to that time by any board or officer of the State. It contained the first full revelation of the working of the law for the registration of vital sta-

[1] *L.*, 1880, c. 151.

tistics. The revelation was a disappointment. Immediately the returns were tabulated it was realized that they were almost valueless. The law required returns both from clerks and health officers in cities, towns and townships. In a total of 428 cities and towns reports had been received from but 72 clerks and 51 health officers, while of the corresponding officers of the 1,637 townships but 413 clerks and 82 health officers had reported.[1] After 1885 the attempt to tabulate and publish elaborate vital statistics was abandoned, and while a perfunctory compliance with the letter of the law was continued, and several attempts made by the Legislature to improve the system, nothing worthy of comment was achieved, and this feature of the board's power remained, what it is to-day, lumber on the statute books—a power that will be hardly worth its printing until it has been subjected to a strong revitalizing force.

The first ten years of the board's existence seem to have been consumed chiefly in making good its title to live. On many hands it met with the coldest indifference and the heaviest apathy, on others with open hostility. There were some legislators wholly opposed to all legislation upon sanitary matters who favored the discontinuance of the State Board of Health, and with it the disbanding of the local boards.[2] Some deemed it little more than a " sinecural title factory." [3]

But by the year 1890 it was less harried by these criticisms and dangers of dissolution, and now it began to push its claims and ask for added powers, for powers at least commensurate with those of the local boards. For what was its rule-making power, its authority to pass a sanitary code, without power to enforce its will or make its opinion

[1] *Report of State Board of Health*, 1885, p. 312.   [2] *Ibid.*, 1887, p. 1.
[3] *Ibid.*, 1899, pp. 429 *et seq.*

felt? It had failed through legislative indifference, opposition or incapacity to gather the facts as to the births and
deaths and conjugal conditions in the State. Must it fail,
too, to get even the faintest recognition of those rules it had
been given such fair-sounding power to pass? In 1885 it
had asked for authority of sanitary supervision of all the
public institutions in the State, and that the officers of such
institutions should be required to report all cases of sickness
and deaths to the board.[1] This suggestion was not considered by the Legislature, but, nothing daunted, the board's
petitions for added powers were reiterated with ever-increas-
ing strength. In 1889 it asked for mandatory authority in
all matters regarding the public health.[2] In 1891 its plea
took a somewhat different form. It asked to be endowed
with the power to abate nuisances and establish and maintain quarantine, but that these powers be exercised only upon
the application of resident citizens " setting forth that, for
any cause, the local board refuses or neglects to properly
protect the people." [3] And to enforce the reasonableness
of this request it was pointed out that there were numerous
instances where the most flagrant violation of sanitary laws,
and even of decency, had taken place, in which, because of
social, business or even political reasons, no redress could
be had through local boards.

Again, and for another season, the desires of the State
Board were disappointed. The State had placed the im-
primatur of superior obligation upon such rules as the
board might devise, and from time to time brought testimony to their paramount authority. In 1892 it had provided that local boards should make such regulations respecting nuisances, sources of filth, causes of sickness, rabid

---

[1] *Report of State Board of Health*, 1885, p. 99.   [2] *Ibid.*, 1889, p. 192.
[3] *Ibid.*, 1891, p. 205.

animals and quarantine, not in conflict with regulations of the State board, as might be necessary, and that the Mayors of cities and towns and the clerks of townships should forthwith without other authority establish quarantine in such cases as might be required by the rules of the State Board of Health and the local boards.[1] Such laws as these were the outward and visible sign of authority, but no more than this. The sign was present but the substance was entirely wanting.

Gradually the need for central authority of less shadowy outlines began to be felt by the people under the stress of experience. By the middle of the decade 1890-1900, and from then on, the applications of citizens to the State board for assistance became numerous. The aid of the State board was asked in removing nuisances caused by stock yards or creameries, to correct abuses connected with slaughter houses, improper sewerage or drainage, hog-pens, unburied dead animals and like sources of offence.[2] But to all this the State board was obliged to turn a deaf ear, permitting itself only to point out that the statute had given it no authority to abate a nuisance or make any order therefor, or enforce a quarantine.

The General Assembly was not so much opposed to an addition of effective authority—though there was beyond a doubt much strenuous protest to any addition—as it was unconvinced of its necessity. Indeed, on occasion it had strengthened the State board in divers minor ways. In 1898, in the law to prevent adulteration and deception in the sale of linseed or flaxseed oils, and to regulate their sale, the State Board of Health was empowered to make rules for the enforcement of the act, and it was provided that the board, its inspectors, assistants, experts and chemists, and others appointed by it, should have access to all

[1] *L.*, 1892, c. 59.   [2] *Report of State Board of Health*, 1897, p. 69.

places where such oils were kept for sale or stored or manufactured.[1]   At the next session it was provided that the
board should determine the number of inspectors of petroleum, not to exceed fourteen, who were to be appointed by
the Governor.[2]   And the board was empowered to make
rules and regulations for the inspection of petroleum products and for the government of inspectors, and it was given
authority to prescribe the instruments and apparatus to be
used.   Another of the minor authorities thus added was
that whereby the board might prescribe the rules for the
distribution among the medical schools of the State of bodies
from poor houses, asylums and similar institutions.[3]   These
things all indicated that the fixity of the board would not
again be assailed, that in the development of the State and
new State functions it filled an important place, from which
even the narrowest policy would not be likely to dislodge it.

At last, in 1902, it was made a central power—a State
administrative authority with the right to direct and demand of the local administration the observance of its will.
This was accomplished, however, not through any coddling
of the legislative favor, but through a striking object lesson
in public catastrophe and sinister inefficacy of the law.
Small-pox had broken out in different parts of the State
for several years preceding the winter of 1902, and each
year it appeared to be on the increase.[4]   In 1902 it took
on unusual and what to outsiders seemed threatening proportions.   In the city of Des Moines, with a population of
over 62,000, it was estimated that there were several hundred cases at one time.   The disease came early in the
winter and remained well into the spring.   Yet there was
much reluctance and slackness in the enforcement of the

[1] *L.*, 1898, c. 52.   [2] *L.*, 1900, c. 83.
[3] *Code*, 1897, § 4946, as amended, *L.*, 1900, c. 129.
[4] *Report of State Board of Health*, 1901, pp. 34, 36.

quarantine laws. This was due to several causes. When the disease first broke out in Des Moines a heavy expense was incurred in quarantining. This made the matter odious to the city council. And as it soon appeared that the disease was of a very mild type, there being almost no deaths from it, the quarantine was in many instances relaxed and indifference prevailed. That the mortality was so low medical experts have explained as due to the fact that the people of the community and their parents had been vaccinated. Among the Indians at the agency the mortality was between 13 and 14 per cent. Many other parts of the State were visited.

But this enormous per cent. of disease to population in the chief city of the State soon attracted attention from abroad. It awakened almost national interest. The apprehension on the part of the city of Chicago was especially strong, so strong indeed that there were threats of discontinuance of business relations with Des Moines. The State Legislature was now in session in the city. It saw that the city council was prone to disregard the advice of the State Board of Health, until the city had been given what was almost an ultimatum from the Health Commissioner of Chicago. The National government took a hand. An agent from the Marine Hospital service made representations and suggestions in the case. The Postoffice Department ordered the mails fumigated at Des Moines. And now for several days the churches, the public library and, nominally, the theatres, were closed. It would hardly need more than this, when enacted under their very eyes, to induce any legislative body to take action. And this the General Assembly did, and gave the State Board of Health full power itself to put its rules and regulations into operation in any community neglecting to observe them. Thus under the pressure of manifest need central control was established in this branch of the administration.

It is not alone in the boards of health, State and local, that centralization of the administration of the public health and safety has developed. The State has assumed certain auxiliary functions which have contributed to this end, in the control of cattle diseases, in the inspection of mines, and the inspection of milk and milk products. We may now trace the development of the administration in these directions.

Previous to 1884 statutory provisions for the care of cattle diseases were practically wanting. Such regulations as were made and enforced were in general customary or a part of the local health regulations. They were very meagre. Horses, mules and asses diseased with nasal gleet, glanders or button farcy running at large without any known owner might be taken before a justice of the peace, and upon his order be destroyed and buried,[1] and police officers and officers of societies for the prevention of cruelty to animals, or magistrates might destroy any horse or other animal disabled and unfit for further use.[2] These were not exactly health regulations, but they were about all the State had with regard to animals at the time.

The creation of the office of State Veterinary Surgeon, like the State Board of Health, was founded upon a Governor's message. But the State Veterinarian may be said to have existed in fact before he did in law, and this, too, through the instrumentality of the Governor. The office was created in 1884. For two years the Governor had received many calls from different parts of the State for the services of some man skilled in the diseases of horses and cattle, competent to check the spread of glanders and pleuro-pneumonia. The Governor called upon the professor of veterinary surgery at the State College of Agri-

[1] *Code,* 1873, § 4057; *Code,* 1897, § 5014.
[2] *Code,* 1873, § 1484; *Code,* 1897, § 2339.

culture for services in the matter. In most of the localities visited by him the people willingly paid his expenses and compensation. In the few cases where this was not done the Governor made a small allowance from his contingent fund. Impressed by this experience with the need of a State Veterinary Surgeon, the Governor recommended the establishment of the office in his message of 1884, and that this officer be made a member of the State Board of Health.[1] The suggestion was agreed to and the office was created, the Governor to appoint and remove its incumbent.[2] The State Veterinarian was given supervision of all contagious and infectious diseases among animals in or being driven or transported through the State, and, with the State Board of Health, might make rules and regulations for prevention and suppression of such diseases, such rules to be published and enforced with the concurrence of the Executive Council.

It cannot be said that the authority of the State Veterinary Surgeon has been increased appreciably by law since the institution of the office, though something has been done through the personal influence of the officers themselves. In 1894 in fact a step was taken toward local control when central control might very well have been increased. Provision was then made for the inspection of diseased sheep by county sheep inspectors, who should be appointed by boards of supervisors.[3] The State Veterinary Surgeon has no share in the appointment of these inspectors; they are not directly amenable to him, and only in a general way can he exercise a supervisory influence over them. Another step toward the diffusion of power was taken in 1897, when the Governor was authorized on behalf of the State to accept any rules and regulations prepared by the Secretary of Agriculture of the United States for the eradication of hog

[1] *Gov. Mess.*, 1884, p. 19.   [2] *L.*, 1884, c. 189.   [3] *L.*, 1894, c. 49.

cholera and swine plague.[1] It was provided that the Governor, together with the State Veterinary Surgeon, might co-operate with the government of the United States for the objects of the law.   The chief significance of these provisions lay in the further fact that the inspectors of the bureau of animal industry of the United States Department of Agriculture were given the right of inspection, quarantine and condemnation of animals affected with the hog cholera or swine plague, and sheriffs, constables and other police officers of the State were required to assist them. These latter provisions may have increased the control of animal disease in the State; it is notable that they do not carry an abrogation of State administration, but they very forcibly show the disinclination as yet to lodge wide powers with the State Veterinary Surgeon.   Of a similar import is the law of 1900 creating the State Department of Agriculture.[2] This law provides that the department, among other things, shall investigate reports of the prevalence of contagious diseases among domestic animals, and report the results of the same, together with recommendations for remedies.   But it is to be noted that the State Veterinary Surgeon is a member of the Board of Agriculture.

In the inspection and oversight of mines, primarily conducted for the care and safety of the miners, there has been a transition from local to State control.   Previous to 1880 the function was left to the counties.   The board of supervisors of every county in which coal or other minerals were mined were required to appoint annually an inspector of mines, who was to inspect the atmosphere in such mines, and upon the discovery of choke or fire damps in sufficient quantities to jeopardize the health or life of the employees or miners, he was required to determine the number and capacity of additional entrances or shafts or other means

---

Code, 1897, §§ 2350 *et seq.*   [2] *L.*, 1900, c. 58.

necessary for proper ventilation, or ingress or egress in the case of explosions, or the falling in of the entrance or shaft.[1]

In 1880 it was provided that there should be a State mine inspector, appointed by the Governor with the consent of the Senate, to hold his office for two years, subject, however, to be removed by the Governor for neglect of duty or malfeasance in office.[2] His salary was $1,500. In 1884 it was made $1,700.[3] In 1886 the number of inspectors was raised from one to three, the Governor to divide the State into inspection districts and assign the inspectors to duty in such places as he should deem proper.[4] The salary was reduced to $1,200 per annum. The only further change of importance was that of 1888, providing that the Executive Council should appoint a board of examiners consisting of two practical miners, two mine operators and one mining engineer, this board to examine applicants for certificates as to their ability to inspect mines, and the Governor to make his selections only from the holders of such certificates.[5]

The inspection of milk in cities of a population of over 10,000, now conducted under the supervision and direction of the State, must be regarded as another direction in which the administration of the public health and safety has developed, and, so developing, has brought State control. This is a rather unusual departure in State administration. In most Commonwealths the matter has been left entirely to the cities, be they large or small.

The office of State Dairy Commissioner was created in 1886.[6] The object of its creation was to prevent deception in the manufacture and sale of imitations of butter and cheese. The Commissioner was to be appointed by the Governor with the consent of the Executive Council, though

[1] *L.*, 1872, c. 44; *Code*, 1873, § 1567.

[2] *L.*, 1880, c. 202.   [3] *L.*, 1884, c. 21.

[4] *L.*, 1886, c. 140.   [5] *L.*, 1888, c. 52.   [6] *L.*, 1886, c. 52.

later such consent was not required.[1]   A very liberal appropriation was made for carrying out the act.   But it was
not until 1892 that the authority of the Commissioner was
extended to include the inspection of milk and the granting
of milk permits in the larger cities.[2]

II OPERATION AND RESULTS OF THE ADMINISTRATION

The State Board of Health is composed of four classes
of members, all of whom have professional qualifications.
They are the Attorney-General of the State, the State
Veterinary Surgeon, one civil engineer and seven physicians.   With the exception of the State Veterinary Surgeon the board has been thus constituted from the beginning, the State Veterinary Surgeon being added in 1884.
The term of the seven physicians and the civil engineer is
seven years, expiring at different times.   These members
are appointed and for cause may be removed by the Governor.   Until 1896 there was no restriction other than the
general qualifications.   In that year it was provided that
no one of the physicians thereafter appointed should be a
member of the Faculty of any medical school in the State.[3]
In 1900 a geographical limitation was introduced.   The
State was divided into eight health districts, and it was
enacted that whenever vacancies occur in the board it should
be the duty of the Governor to appoint to membership on
the board physicians residing in the various health districts
until seven districts are represented, after which time the
annual appointment is to be made from the district not
represented the preceding year.[4]   The secretary of the board
is the only salaried member, and he is the board's executive
officer, though the presidency rests elsewhere.   The secre-

[1] *Code*, 1897, § 2515.   [2] *L.*, 1892, c. 50.

[3] *L.*, 1896, c. 91.   [4] *L.*, 1900, c. 88.

tary must be a physician. His salary is determined by the board, but may not exceed $1,200 yearly. The other members of the board receive only their actual traveling and other necessary expenses. The sum at the disposition of the board is limited to $5,000 per year, and from this must come the secretary's salary, the expenses of the board, the contingent expenses of the secretary's office, which is established at the State capital, and all the costs of printing. The statute does not provide for a biologist, chemist or laboratory facilities. The board, however, appoints an official biologist and chemist, whose compensation is met by fees for services performed.

The functions of the board fall into several categories. Its functions with relation to the local boards of health constitute perhaps the most important class. Of secondary, but still of great, importance are those general State health powers that it exercises with the entire Commonwealth as the unit of administration. Embraced in this class are found such powers as regard the distribution of bodies among the medical schools, the publication of circulars, bulletins, etc., and the transportation of corpses. In another group may be placed the powers that it exercises with the State Veterinary Surgeon in controlling cattle disease through its rules and regulations. However, in the execution of such rules the Veterinary Surgeon is entirely independent of the board. Finally, the powers that the board exercises in relation to the inspectors of flaxseed and linseed oils and the inspectors of petroleum are to be distinguished. A still further class might be added, but not without extreme qualification. The medical members of the board constitute the State Board of Medical Examiners, with power to examine all applicants to practice medicine in the State, of whatever kind or school. And though the secretary of the State Board of Health is, moreover, the secretary of the Board of Medical Examiners, the two boards are entirely independent and have no legal identity.

Taking up these powers in their several classes, the first to be commented upon are those found in the relation of the State Board of Health to the local boards. It has been shown what a fiasco was the attempt to secure the registration of vital statistics. And yet had the law been workable, here was one of the most plausible avenues for the gradual upbuilding of administrative strength and harmonious relations between the State and the local health administration. Under the law as it stood at first physicians and midwives were required, under penalty, to report all births and deaths to the clerk of the district court, who, in turn, was to report these facts, together with the county registration of marriages, to the secretary of the State board.[1] In the same law it was required that the official physicians and clerks of the local boards should report their proceedings and such other facts as the State board might require. The law as it now stands supposes this double series of reports, except that the duty of physicians and midwives has been transferred to the local assessors.[2] Under every device yet adopted there has been complexity, lack of real coercive authority, and a duplication of ministerial officers. With so many cooks perhaps we should not wonder that the broth was spoiled.

The second means through which the local boards might have been made amenable to the State board, had the statute been possessed of a little greater vigor, was that providing for the making of rules and regulations by the State board. The power granted was general and with little limit. The board was authorized " to make such rules and regulations, * * as they may from time to time deem necessary for the preservation or improvement of the public

[1] *L.*, 1880, c. 151.   [2] *Code*, 1897, § 2566.

health." But not until 1902 did this become more than
empty legal verbiage. It then became real, and a power that,
if taken full advantage of, may prove to be the corrective
of almost every evil of lax township or city administration.
The law is inclusive. It gives the State board power to
enforce any of its rules and regulations when the local board
neglects or refuses to enforce them, and for that purpose
the board has and may exercise all the powers given by law
to local boards of health, that is, the State board becomes,
as it were, a local board for the time being. The expenses
of such enforcement are to be paid in the same manner as
is provided for the payment of similar expenses of local
boards of health.[1]

This is the important element in the new law. The act
whereby the State board was created provided that its rules
and regulations should be enforced, and gave the board
power, so-called, to demand the assistance of the police
officers and all other officers of the State in securing their
enforcement. Such authority, however, proved futile. It
was narrow, and it did not carry with it the power to make
a charge against the township or city whose health officials
had been delinquent.

A number of States have provided special State funds
for use by the State board when central interference is
necessary, but it would seem that the policy of making a
charge upon the local division were preferable, for it will
make the locality alive to the character of its local board
and alert to see that the regulations are enforced. It is too
early to say what will be the results of this law generally,
but so far it seems to have worked admirably, though it
has operated in most cases rather *in terrorem,* as judges
sometimes say, than by active application. To December 5,
1902, that being the date of the last information obtained

[1] *L.,* 1902, c. 107, and *Code,* 1897, § 2571.

by the writer, it had been necessary to use this authority in but two cases. In these cases the president of the board says, "Authority was delegated to some competent and judicious physician to do the work at the instance of the State board. It was effectively done, and no wrangling or litigation grew out of the exercise of this authority. It was exercised only in cases of palpable neglect, and left no opportunity for litigation. The fact that such power could be and would be used was sufficient." [1]

The secretary of the State Board of Health, as its executive officer, has been frequently called upon to render personal assistance to local boards, to State institutions or to individual petitioners. Such questions as correct diagnosis or the determination of causes of disease in special circumstances frequently come before him.

There appears to have been little effort whose direct aim and principal purpose were to secure the organization of local boards. But we find little complaint upon that score at any time in the history of the State board. One of the earliest criticisms was, not that there was failure to organize, but that there was failure to report when organized.[2] In 1883 it was complained that not one-half of the organized local boards had reported. It is now asserted that there are almost no cases where organization has not been effected. Sometimes the fact that there has been no organization will transpire. Usually it is brought to light by some local officer attempting to exercise a power which can be legally exercised only by a health officer or member of a board of health or its agent. Such officer will be taken to task, and in many cases organization will speedily follow.

Of the health functions exercised by the State board independently of the local boards the one that has developed

[1] *Letter from Dr. A. M. Linn,* President of the State Board of Health.
[2] *Report of State Board of Health,* 1883, p. 129.

into the greatest influence is that of publication of circulars and the dissemination of information concerning sanitation, hygiene or the diagnosis and the cure of disease. In 1887 the *Iowa Health Bulletin,* published by the State board, began its career. Several thousand copies of this journal are issued and distributed every month free of charge to all the local boards, to interested physicians and others. The information collated in this journal, as well as that in the special circulars, is directed both to the people and to the medical profession. During the small-pox pest, for instance, a circular was prepared describing the small-pox in untechnical terms, so as to enable any one to detect it.

Among other State-wide functions of importance is that relating to the transportation of bodies of persons dying of infectious disease. The State Board of Health was one of the first to adopt rules whereby bodies of those dying of diphtheria, scarlet fever, glanders, anthrax or leprosy could be transported, and, so it is stated, it was the first to provide for the examination and licensing of embalmers.[1] Within the last few years a number of States have enacted laws providing for such examinations. The authority of the Iowa board came about in a different way, and in the development of that authority the fertile strength of the rule-making power of the board is well displayed. The board had sought of the General Assembly direct legislation for the examination and licensing of embalmers. But this it failed to obtain, whereupon the opinion of the Attorney-General was requested as to the board's powers. He replied that he believed it within the board's competence to legislate in the matter. Accordingly it proceeded to the adoption of the appropriate rules and regulations. And under the rules so adopted, without special legislative action and, so far, without judicial endorsement or reprobation, the examination

[1] *Report of State Board of Health,* 1901, p. 78.

of embalmers has continued. This is administrative legislation. Its force depends somewhat upon a third party—
the transportation companies, which have been authorized
and have agreed to transport bodies coming from the licensed
embalmers. The rules went into effect September 1, 1898,
and by June 30, 1901, four hundred and sixty-six embalmers' licenses had been issued.

Little can be gathered from statistics to show what has
been the effect of the health administration upon the death
rate and the general sanitary conditions of the State. This
is due to the deplorable puerility of the several laws for the
collection of vital statistics. As has been shown, none worth
publication have as yet been gathered.[1] The formidable
compilations of uncertainties and statistical guess-work
made according to law are allowed to rest in the cabinets
of the State board undisturbed. For they are well nigh
valueless. They are certainly misleading.

The method usually employed to test sanitary conditions
as modified by health administration is the comparison of
the zymotic death rates over different periods or the zymotic
death rates combined with the rates in diseases which are
most subject to control by sanitary regulations. But nothing of the kind is, as yet, possible in Iowa. Not only is this
so with regard to the State as a whole, but it cannot be
attempted even in the registration cities. Of the seven
registration cities in Iowa in 1900, which were Burlington,
Davenport, Keokuk, Marshalltown, Muscatine, Oskaloosa,
Ottumwa and Sioux City, only three provided for registration in 1890, or gathered data sufficient to justify an
estimate of the death rate. These three were Davenport,
Keokuk and Muscatine. And little can be gathered from
such isolated instances. The comparison of the general

---

[1] For argument of the State board on this matter, see especially its reports for 1895
pp. 345, 346, and 1901, pp. 108, 109.

death rate in these three cities makes this sufficiently evident.
In Davenport it was 16.4 in 1890 and 15.9 in 1900.   There
was thus a decrease.   But in the other two cities there was
an increase.   In Keokuk the rate was 14.7 in 1890 and 19.1
in 1900; in Muscatine 15.7 in 1890 and 17.1 in 1900.[1]   The
matter must be left in doubt until an adequate system of
registration has been perfected.   But there seems to be
ample ground for assuming that the system of State and
local boards has contributed greatly to the improvement
of the sanitary conditions.   Outbreaks of disease or un-
toward sanitary conditions have usually, though by no means
universally, been conspicuous by their absence.   Still more
may be expected from the added powers that have been
conferred upon the State board.

Of the State board's functions in conjunction with the
State Veterinary Surgeon, in which a third class of powers
has been roughly grouped, little will be said here.   It is
sufficient to note that the power to make rules and regulations for the suppression and prevention of cattle diseases
enables the State board to obtain added light upon its primary duty—the preservation of human health.   The recent
controversy concerning the relation of tuberculosis in cattle
to tuberculosis in human beings illustrates this.

The relations of the State board to the inspection of flaxseed and linseed oils and the inspection of petroleum products are also of minor importance.   As regards the particular interests involved, however, they are very significant,
for the board has power to determine the number of
inspectors, not exceeding the statutory limit, that shall be
appointed by the Governor,[2] and also has powers to make
rules and regulations for and prescribe methods of inspection.[3]   The State board is given a very close control over

---

[1] *Twelfth Census of the United States*, vol. ii, part i, p. lx.

[2] *Code*, 1897, § 2503.   [3] *L.*, 1898, c. 52.

the inspection and regulation of the sale of linseed and flaxseed oil. Violation of any of the provisions of the act relating to the manufacture and adulteration of linseed or flaxseed oil is declared to be a public nuisance, and any court of competent jurisdiction is authorized upon the application of the State board or its agents to enjoin the violation. And it is made the duty of the county attorney upon the application of the State board to conduct the prosecution. But the board has been indisposed to press legal proceedings when the county attorney or oil inspector has recommended that they should not be pressed. The board has expressed its belief that enforcement of the provisions of the act, further than the duty of determining the quality of the oil, should not be placed upon it, and the secretary has expressed the belief that the testing of such oils is not the appropriate work of a sanitary body.[1]

The State Board of Medical Examiners and the State Board of Health, though legally distinct, have a close relation. And this relation has an important bearing upon the health administration. For in the hands of the board of medical examiners is placed the power of granting and revoking licenses of physicians. There are numerous cases where physicians, through ignorance or a desire to shield patients, fail to report to the proper health officers cases of contagious disease subject to quarantine. In some of these cases the board has disciplined physicians, but the statute gives it power to revoke certificates only in the case of bad moral character, habitual intoxication, lack of qualification, incompetency or fraud in procuring the certificate, and as yet these causes have not been interpreted by the courts to include delinquency in reporting contagious disease. This being the case, a definite law upon the subject

[1] *Report of State Board of Health*, 1901, p. 21.

granting the board power to suspend and revoke certificates in such cases has been recommended.[1]

The organization of the auxiliary health administration, the veterinary department, the mine inspection and the milk and dairy inspection, is shown to a great extent in the discussion of the historical development. Here we need add but a few details, with some comments as to results.

The position of the State Veterinary Surgeon has an unstable basis. Not because the control of cattle diseases is an authority in which single-headed and centralized responsibility would be unwise, but because it has been the victim of legislative chances and of the expedients of indifference, it has been spread out thin over so many offices. For the care and regulation of cattle diseases is now reposed' in no less than five sets of officers, in the State Board of Health, in the Governor, in the officers of the United States Department of Agriculture, in the county sheep inspectors, and finally in the State Veterinary Surgeon. To this list might be added, with some limitations, the State Department of Agriculture, the Executive Council and the justices of the peace. This system of diffusion of responsibility has taken advantage of constituted organs, but in many cases such decentralization must have meant a sacrifice rather than a saving. The theory of governmental checks has been carried to an extreme in the provision that the Executive Council shall concur in the rules and regulations for the control of cattle diseases, as adopted by the Veterinary Surgeon and the State Board of Health.

The compensation of the Veterinary Surgeon is five dollars per day and expenses while actually engaged in the discharge of his duties. In cases of emergency the Governor may appoint assistants or substitutes. The annual expenditure for this service is limited to $3,000 per year.

[1] *Report of State Board of Health*, 1901, p. 80.

The point worthy of most attention in the law for the inspection of mines is found in the new powers that State as against local administration brought with it. With the transfer of the duty and power to the State there came a broadening in the functions and authority of the inspectors. For instance, when the mine inspector finds the air insufficient or the men working under unsafe conditions, he is required to give notice thereof to the mine owner or agent, and upon failure to make the necessary changes he may order the men out, to remain out until the mine is put in proper condition.[1] Furthermore, while under the local administration failure to observe the requirements of the inspectors simply made the mine owner answerable in " full damages " to the person injured or his family,[2] under the State administration the inspector, in addition to all other remedies, may obtain an injunction against the continued working of the mine when the requisite appliances are not provided.[3] The power to test the oils used in mines for illuminating purposes and require that they reach a certain standard is another authority that has come, though rather more recently, with the change in the administrative system. The State Board of Health is empowered to fix the standard of purity and establish regulations for the testing of oils. For a short time the inspection was made by the mine inspectors,[4] but now it is made by inspectors of petroleum products.[5]

The State Dairy Commissioner, like the mine inspectors, the Veterinary Surgeon and the members of the Board of Health, is required to possess special qualifications. He must have " a practical knowledge of and experience in the manufacture of dairy products." He is allowed a salary of $1,500 per year, and must devote all of his time to the work

---

[1] *Code*, 1897, § 2488.   [2] *Code*, 1873, § 1568.   [3] *Code*, 1897, § 2492.
[4] *Ibid.*, 1897, § 2945.   [5] *L.*, 1898, c. 60.

of his office. His position is unique among those branches of the administration in which are found both local and central officers. To the extent that the State has authority over the local milk supply, its regulation and inspection, it is entirely central control. The local inspectors are appointed by the State Dairy Commissioner, and are answerable to him alone. They are subject neither to city council nor county board of supervisors. But it is to be remembered that the jurisdiction is limited. It applies only to cities having a population over 10,000. In 1901 there were fourteen cities within this class in the State, their aggregate population amounting to about sixteen per cent. of that of the entire State.

There is one inspector in each of these cities. He is payable at the rate of $3.00 per day for each day that he is employed. In no case does he work less than three days in each month, while in Des Moines, where more than one-fourth of the total permits are issued, he works on an average of fourteen days. At first samples were sent to the State Dairy Commissioner himself for inspection, but with the introduction of the Babcock test this has become unnecessary. However, monthly reports of the inspections are made to the Commissioner, so he is enabled to keep a careful lookout for cases falling below the minimum grade. Indeed, the power of the Commissioner himself to inspect and administer the law is in no wise diminished by the existence of these agents. He, as well as his inspectors, may open any can or vessel in which milk or cream is offered for sale in one of the cities in the class concerned. And he has the power, very often refused to administrative officers, to subpœna witnesses, enforce their attendance and examine them under an oath administered by himself.

If we place the several branches of the administration of health and safety side by side and notice their relations, the one to the other, the conspectus will cause several important facts immediately to appear. It becomes apparent that the State Board of Health is the paramount authority. The State board is seen to touch every branch of the health administration with the exception of the dairy and milk inspection. It touches them through its legislative authority, that is, its power to make rules and regulations. This is the chief source of its power, but the several branches feel its administrative influence as well, the local boards of health in their liability to the State administrative action should they neglect the rules and regulations of the State board, the several inspectors of oils, petroleum and mines in their obligation to heed the rules of the board, and in various incidents of administrative power. However, the State Veterinary Surgeon, though the rules that he enforces are the rules of the State board, is, so far as the State board is concerned, an independent executive agent. Almost as much is to be said of the mine inspectors.

Another prime fact is that all the officers in this department of administration are appointed by the Governor, and are removable by him. With the exception of the members of the State Board of Health not otherwise officers of the State, whose term is seven years, the term of office is short, generally two years; in the case of the State Veterinary Surgeon three. This means a large measure of executive direction and control.

In any forecast of the future of the health administration it should be remembered that the tendency of recent legislation has been to bestow even greater powers upon the State Board of Health, both in its relation to the general State administration, whether it concern immediately or remotely the public health, and in its power over the local boards. It should also be observed that this has been done without increasing the material equipment of the board, without providing for assistants, or longer or more properly executive sessions of the board. Five thousand dollars remains the limit of the appropriation. There are as yet no laboratory facilities and no official chemist or biologist. It would seem that the future of health administration generally is to be in the direction of greater scientific investigation. Modern research has shown that nuisances and filth have comparatively little causative relation to disease,[1] yet, as we have seen, the health administration in its earliest form in Iowa took the direction of the abatement of nuisances, and in that form has occupied a large part of the law to the present time. But now the road seems turning; with it the demand for greater facilities for scientific investigation and experiment are met with. Thus the need for laboratory facilities, the need for central strength to exercise the powers now given the State board to enforce its rules, and the gradual accumulation of many minor functions in its hands—these things all point toward the need of upbuilding at the center. The powers have received a wise extension and circumscription. The material tools now remain to be provided. In some other branches of the health administration, particularly in the care of cattle diseases, where authority is held in so many hands, and where consolidation would appear to be of advantage, there may appear opportunities for improvement, but, as a whole, it is to be said that the administration of public health and safety has been wisely organized.

[1] *New York State Library Bulletin*, no. 72, p. 157.

CHAPTER V

PUBLIC FINANCE: INCOME AND ADMINISTRATION

I GENERAL CHARACTER OF THE INCOME ADMINISTRATION

THE study of the income administration of the State of Iowa, and of its finance administration generally, is instructive not so much for what it now is as for what it has been. As a development it is of striking suggestiveness. But the product of that development is not what might have been expected. We shall find in the history of this administration, in the interplay of harmonious or antagonistic forces that have worked now to the peaceful sustenance of the State, now to heated ferments in courts, Legislatures and political conventions, a drama of the controversies of the day. The question of segregation, that is, of the separation of State and local sources of revenue, the question of central or local assessments, the questions of uniformity and equality of burdens, all of these have at one time or another occupied the center of the stage, and one by one they have to a large degree been thrust back by the iron discipline of judicial interpretation, by the indifference of the people or their representatives, or by the manipulations of the supple agents of special interests.

To-day the financial system of Iowa, like that of the great majority of the States, offers but a bleak prospect to the searcher for evidences of advancement in financial institutions. Here and there he does encounter something that

159]   159

commends itself to his opinion, the inheritance tax, or the
State assessment of the values of non-local public service
corporations, but these are almost overborne by the dead
level of the general property tax, which has stretched its
paralyzing influence over all forms of value alike. But
there was a time in the history of the State when there
seemed every promise of a separation of State and local
revenues, and State equalization not only as between counties
but as between towns as well, not only as between real property values but as between personal values also, these and
other measures of advancement. Because of these facts,
then, our study of the income administration will be more
preponderatingly historical than has been that of the school,
the institutional or the health administration, and we shall
content ourselves with only a brief examination of the system of to-day.

There is no branch of the administration so difficult, none
so involved, as the financial. So multitudinous is the machinery of that administration, so various its parts, that we
may speak of centralization or decentralization and mean
any one of half a dozen things if we do not take the pains
to define the connotation of the moment. For this reason
it is necessary that a plan somewhat rigidly systematic be
pursued in the treatment of this branch of the subject.

First we shall take a brief historical survey of the beginnings of the finances down to and including the Code of
1851. There will then follow a detailed analysis of the
specific movements that begin with the middle of the century, of the rise and decline of segregation, of State assessment, of State equalization and of State direction of the
local administration. And a final section will discuss the
correlation of the various processes of centralization or
decentralization, and the possible remedies for present defects. The first two divisions will supplement the one the

other. Both will be historical. The reasons for particular discussion of segregation, State assessment, State equalization and State supervision of local administration will readily appear as the reader progresses. It will be seen that in them are wrapped up practically all the problems of the finance administration, and more especially those of centralization.

II HISTORICAL SURVEY OF STATE TAXES AND STATE TAX ADMINISTRATION, 1834-1860

In the year 1834 Iowa was redeemed from that peculiar condition of civil neglect which had left it almost a forgotten land on the outskirts of a vigorous government, a land over which, though a part of the United States, a President of the United States refused to exercise authority, believing he had none.[1] In the year 1834 it was given a civil status. It was made a part of the territory of Michigan. Prior to this time, it seems, no taxes had been levied.[2] Whatever sums were needed for the execution of the rude squatter government of the day were raised by voluntary contribution. In a day when without any lawful court to try civil causes or criminal complaints, the self-constituted tribunals of the people assumed to condemn even to death, then raised the costs of the trial by popular collection,[3] financial practice and financial administration of course had no place.

But with the territorial Constitution there was at least a law for taxation, whether there was any substantial levy and collection or not. Beginning with this new era in 1834 and extending to the year 1851, when the first code was adopted, we have a period that, corresponding somewhat to the earliest period in the school administration, we may describe

[1] See Macy *op. cit.*, p. 350.
[2] See F. H. Noble, *Taxation in Iowa*, p. 10.
[3] Macy, *op. cit.*, p. 350.

as one of pronounced decentralization. The taxes during this time are of the nature of general property taxes, poll taxes or license fees. And their administration is at no time given any modicum of very effective central control. In the early years of the period the central State government is, in the matter of contributions, almost left to the mercy of the local divisions, so loose is the law.

Of prime importance in the first twelve years of this period is the territorial status. For during the territorial period the government is supported in chief, though not entirely, by the national purse. This fact promotes an unhealthy torpor. The central territorial government is to a degree careless of the financial enginery of the local. It expects little from it, and, as if it were not worth while, is indisposed to make fast that little. In 1838, after having passed from under the overlordship of Michigan, then been severed from the Wisconsin territory and government and made a territory by itself, Congress, to launch the new government, granted the sum of $24,675, out of which the civil list, the expenses of the Legislative Assembly and the printing of the laws and taking of the census were to be paid. Congress also made appropriations for territorial buildings, a penitentiary and a library, part of which it augmented from time to time, while it continued its appropriations in ever-increasing amounts for the support of the territorial government. But apparently the sums were not adequate to the needs of the territory, for the treasury was continually running behind, and the messages of the Governors continually demanding an economical administration.[1] It can hardly be said that the financial administration of the territory was a success. This is imputable to several causes. If the tirades of many who voiced contemporary sentiment on this matter, or even the milder criticisms of

[1] See *Gov. Mess.*, *H. J.*, 1840–41, p. 12; *Ibid.*, 1841–42, p. 15.

executive messages are to be accepted, it was largely due
to the parsimony of the National government.[1] Especially
was the government accused of failure to make adequate
appropriations for the penitentiary that it had fathered. A
second cause is found in the failure of the counties to pay
over to the Territorial Treasurer their proportion of the
territorial levy. The first year of the separate territorial
existence only $138.07 was paid into the treasury, while
the amount of the arrears of taxes, as far as the counties
had reported assessment rolls—and a number had wholly
failed to do so—was $442.66.[2] This might have been
attributable in part to the peculiar law of the day, which
provided not that the revenue from the counties should be
based upon a territorial levy, but that the county treasurer
should be required to pay over to the territory five per cent.
of the taxes levied by the board of county commissioners.[3]
The further provision that this sum should be paid out of the
first collection probably had little significance   But in 1841
this law was repealed, and it was provided in lieu thereof
that one-fourth of a mill should be levied for territorial
purposes.[4] Still the arrears continued. In some cases
counties gave not the slightest heed to the law, and financial
officers and Governors alike united in scoring these delinquencies and the income system that made them possible.[5]
Several steps were indeed taken to remedy this defect, but
they were all petty half measures—the county treasurer
was required to collect the tax [6] or county clerk to transmit

[1] *Gov. Mess., C. J.*, 1842–43, pp. 9, 10; *Ibid., C. J.*, 1843–44, pp. 8–10.

[2] *Auditor's Report, H, J.*, 1840–41, p. 28.   [3] *L.*, 1838–39, Jan. 25, 1839.

[4] *L.*, 1840–41, c. 90.

[5] *Auditor's Report, C. J.*, 1843–44, pp. 241, 242; *Gov. Mess., C. J.*, 1845–46,
p. 18.

[6] *L.*, 1844, c. 21. Under a previous law the tax was collected by a county
collector, elected annually. *L.*, 1842–43, Act Feb. 13, 1843.

the aggregate valuation of the county to the State Auditor,[1] etc.,—and all fell short of the mark.   It is possible that some of the blame for the failure to balance income and expenditure is to be attributed to the pioneer law-makers themselves, for we find numerous recommendations for shorter sessions, for the making of appropriations " more specific," and like remedies, but there is little palpable evidence to shatter their now long-established reputation for careful expenditure.

Things had come to such a pass in 1845 that the treasurer could report that territorial warrants were worth but fifty cents on the dollar,[2] a depreciation that was scarcely to be found in any county of the territory, which though it could be traced in part to the creation of a debt of $8,650, for the constitutional convention of the year préceding, was a sharp commentary on the shortcomings of the finances.   And when the State was admitted into the Union in 1846 it came burdened with a debt of about $20,000, not a large sum, but one sufficient to inspire many misgivings in a time of pioneer hardships and to make some enter dubiously upon the new era of State government.[3]

There had been those who had opposed the assumption of a State constitution and governmental autonomy largely because of reluctance to meet the burdens which the new form would impose,[4] and this attitude had been successful in delaying for a time the adoption of a State Constitution,[5] but now when at last the die was cast, when it was apparent that the old debt was not to be sloughed off upon the National government and that new exigencies were to arise, those

[1] *L.*, 1844, c. 29.

[2] *Treasurer's Report, C. J.*, 1845–46, p. 255.

[3] *Gov. Mess., H. J.*, 1846–47, p. 14.

[4] *Gov. Mess., C. J.*, 1845, p. 14.

[5] Benjamin F. Shambaugh, *History of the Constitutions of Iowa*, pp. 167 *et seq.*, 260.

in responsible positions began to turn their eyes to the ways and means of providing. The gubernatorial message to the first State Legislature breathed the spirit of vigorous inquiry and resolution to upbuild a sound finance. It is one of the very few messages that contains anything novel or original in financial recommendation. The Governor recommended that in order to meet the costs of the State government without at the same time too greatly increasing the general burden a reduction be made in the costs of the county and township by introducing greater simplicity in their government, by combining offices, by requiring clerks, sheriffs and others to transact the county business without fees, and dispensing with the *per diem* of grand jurors. He also recommended a tax upon suits brought in the district court of the State " as furnishing a legitimate and reliable source of revenue." Of the general property tax he made no criticism, saying that he believed the inequality and lack of uniformity complained of were as much due to the selection of incompetent and improper agents to execute the laws as to any defect in the system itself. The Governor in general terms called for the application of a wide and searching reform, but the character of that reform he left to the ingenuity of the Legislature.[1] He gave no hint as to its outline; probably he had none to give.

But if much was to be expected from the new order, the disappointment was complete, for there was practically no change of note from the taxation of the territorial period. Property, polls and licenses continued the bases. The rate of State levy was naturally increased. It was made two mills on the dollar. A few years afterwards it was increased to three mills,[2] but in the later history of the State it has not tended to go beyond this. Indeed, it has been much

[1] *Gov. Mess., H. J.*, 1846–47, pp. 12–18.

[2] *Code*, 1851, § 454.

less in many years.[1]   Assessment was to be by the county
sheriff, who was made *ex officio* county assessor.   But this
was not of stable significance.   In 1853 change was made
to township assessors.[2]   In 1844 the assessment had been
by township or, when there were no township, by precinct
assessors.[3]   The year following a regular county assessor
was to be elected for the purpose.[4]   And now in 1847 the
duty was superimposed upon the police duties of a police
officer.

In the matter of local equalization the law of 1847 showed
at least a dim consciousness of the desirability of local
review.   But it was as yet rather a remedy for the aggrieved
tax-payer than a function that should in all cases be performed by the local government of its own motion.   It was
provided merely that the county commissioners should examine the assessment rolls and hear and decide upon applications for abatement.

The most important of these unimportant variations from
the territorial system was, however, the transfer of the tax
on peddlers from the county to the State.   Under this law
there was to be collected for State purposes a tax of twenty-
five dollars on every hawker or peddler of goods, wares
and merchandise for the privilege of peddling throughout
the State for one year.   The tax was uniform for all such
" pedlars," except the peddler of clocks, who had been made
the special prey of these license fees from the first, and was
now charged fifty dollars per year, something less than he
had to pay under previous laws.[5]   This departure is de-

---

[1] The highest rate levied from 1879 to 1898 inclusive, was 2.9 mills.   In the
great majority of cases it was 2 mills.

[2] *L.*, 1852–53, c. 69.   The State Auditor, however, strongly recommended change
to county assessors in 1856.   *Auditor's Report*, 1856, p. 161.

[3] *L.*, 1843–44, c. 21.   [4] *L.*, 1845, c. 5.

[5] *L.*, 1846–47, c. 100.   Subsequently these fees were increased somewhat.

scribed as of relative importance, not because it meant the shifting of a large fund of revenue from one order of government to another, for the product of the tax was always insignificant, but because it is the first definite step in the segregation of State and local revenues. True this revenue had been left to the counties before, but the facts of the territorial status and the insignificance of the tax forbid the attachment of any import to it. This feature of the law of 1847 was the beginning of segregation, an almost unwitting and feeble beginning, one to which the subsequent accomplishments in this direction owed no impetus, but yet it is worthy of attention as evidence of the fact that the State thus early was not necessarily bound by any devotion to uniformity of system for both State and local government.

There was almost no financial discussion and little change from now on until the Code of 1851 became law. But with the Code of 1851 well-nigh revolutionary changes in the organs of county administration, and so in the local administration of the income, were made. There were also sweeping alterations in the taxing system, both in the bases of taxes and in the machinery of their administration. Previous thereto the county was ruled by a board of three county commissioners; now it was placed under a single-man power, the county judge system. Previously there had been no State equalization, now a State board of equalization was created. Until this code there had been no such thing as distinct corporation taxes. The word corporation had hardly been mentioned in the revenue laws, and when it was mentioned it was by way of recitation and not of differentiation that it appeared.[1] But now the shares of

[1] This is subject to slight qualification. During the brief period when Iowa was subject to Michigan, express provision was made for the taxation of stocks in banks, insurance companies and other corporations, and the manner of assessment

bank stocks were expressly made subject to taxation.[1] Insurance companies incorporated outside of the State, doing
business within it, were to be assessed one per cent. for
State purposes and one per cent. for county purposes on
the premiums received in the separate counties.[2] And,
more important, the property of corporations or companies
constructing canals, railroads and " similar improvements "
were to be taxed through the " shares of the stockholders." [3]
Up to this time the Legislatures had gone upon the hypothesis that the individual holder of a corporate security
would list the same as he did his other personal property,
and had left corporations inferentially to the more than
tender mercies of the general property law. But now such
overweening confidence was done away with, and there was
express provision for corporation taxation.

The Code of 1851 is justly famous. Seldom has a body
of laws introduced so many and such extraordinary innovations. Its chief title to fame lies in the fact that it marked
the abandonment of the common law and the adoption of
the code system, and in the fact that it was one of the earliest
of the American codes. But among its many remarkable
provisions the revenue measures are not the least. And
what renders them the more curious is that they passed the
Legislature and were launched upon their course without
let or hindrance. They were almost undiscussed by the
general public,[4] and while the same thing may be said of

was much like that of the present day. See *Laws of the Territory of Michigan*,
arranged and passed by the Fifth Legislative Council, 1833, p. 88. Affected by
Act approved Feb. 20, 1834, *Territorial Laws of Michigan*, vol. iii, p. 1270.

    [1] *Code*, 1851, § 456.   [2] *Ibid.*, § 464.   [3] *Ibid*, § 462.

    [4] The *Democratic Enquirer*, of Muscatine, Ia., on Jan. 18, 1851, reviewing the
proposals of the new code, mentions as important the usury laws, the license question, the individual liability clause in the general incorporation act, and says:
" These are the most important changes proposed," thus showing how little significance was attached to the new revenue measures.

about all the provisions of the code,[1] it is to be wondered at
most in taxation, which affects so intimately the interests
and the passions of the people. But this was in general
a period of apathy in revenue discussion. Not since 1846,
when the retiring territorial Governor had expressed his
earnest wish that a system might be devised whereby the
rigors, the inequality, of the revenue laws should be reduced,
had any Governor given much attention to the subject.
The same is to be said, though not with equal inclusiveness,
of the general financial officers [2] and, as it would appear,
of the press of the State. It is not surprising in the lack
of discussion that when nine years later the continuance
of the county judge system was under debate there should
be those who would assert that the people in the adoption
of the system, as in other features of the code, had been
imposed upon.[3] The people had not in fact been imposed
upon. Nothing had been done by stealth. But when in
the operation of new organs and new laws they came to
realize that here was a thing they had never discussed, had
never expressed an opinion of, pro or con, the fact that they
had slept while the law was born made it seem to some of
them that they had perhaps been outwitted and wronged.
But the measures of the code were in general satisfactory.
It was only in a few instances that they provoked rebellion.

[1] The Iowa City correspondent of the *Democratic Enquirer*, on Dec. 21, 1850,
reviewed briefly the proposed change in the county administration, and expressed
himself as in favor of it, his chief reason seeming to be that, as he thought, it provided for the submission of all important questions to the direct vote of the people
of the county. And yet the papers usually passed the matter over without more
than the briefest reference to the fact that there was such action. And, see *The
Iowa Star*, of Des Moines, Ia., issue of Jan. 2, 1851.

[2] Such recommendations as they had made, looked more to the perfection of
the detail of the administration than any basic reform. *Auditor's Report, H.
J.*, 1850–51, p. 6.

[3] *Iowa City Republican*, Feb. 29, 1860.

Both in the school administration and in the administration of charities and corrections we have glanced at the county judge, and in either place we might have discussed the office at some length. But it is more in the financial functions that the importance and peculiarity of the office is evinced, and hence our slight examination may be made with more profit here.

Previous to the Code of 1851 the county had been administered by a board of three commissioners chosen at large from the county, the commissioner system dating from the Wisconsin act of December 20, 1837.[1] Under the Michigan territorial laws the supervisor system had been in operation, that is, the county was governed by a board of supervisors consisting of one elected from each township.[2] In 1834 the territory which had previously constituted but one county was divided at the lower end of Rock Island, by a line running therefrom through to the Missouri River, into a northern and a southern half, each of which was made a county, the northern being named Dubuque, the southern Demoine [*sic*].[3] Each of these counties was constituted a single township for purposes of local government. With the passage under the Wisconsin government a still further division was made. Des Moines county was cut up into seven counties,[4] Dubuque into fourteen.[5] Shortly before the division of Des Moines county a system that was assimilated to the commissioner system, in a large measure, had been

[1] *Laws of the Territory of Wisconsin*, 1836–38, p. 138.

[2] *Laws of the Territory of Michigan*, vol. ii, p. 583, Act April 12, 1897 (and see vol. ii, p. 317, Act March 30, 1827), abolishing the system of three commissioners appointed by the Governor, as created by Act May 8, 1820; *Ibid.*, vol. I, p. 661.

[3] *Engrossed Laws of the Territory of Michigan*, Act Sept. 6, 1834.

[4] *Laws of the Territory of Wisconsin*, 1836–38, p. 78, Act Dec. 7, 1836.

[5] *Ibid.*, p. 132, Act Dec. 31, 1837.

formally adopted.[1]   This was further confirmed and made
specific,[2] and it continued from now on till 1851, but not
without deviations of some importance.   By special acts
a number of counties were empowered to district themselves and provide for the election of commissioners, one
from each district.[3]   In 1847, indeed, it was provided that
all counties in the State might be divided into county commissioner districts [4] and commissioners be elected from the
districts, but this did not mean that they must adopt the
system of local representation.   It was merely an authori-
zation, to be followed or not, as the county pleased.

The Code of 1851 now gave the county judge the powers
that had been exercised by the commissioners, and, moreover, the powers of probate judges.   From the beginning
of its distinct organization the territory had had a separate
probate judge for each county.[5]   This may be accounted
for by the organic law itself, which apparently contemplated the creation of probate courts that should be distinct
from the Supreme Court, district courts and the justices of
the peace.   The creation of the office of county judge was
not a displacement of the office of probate judge, but an
extension of that office.   The commissioners, rather, were
the officers dislodged.

The county judge had almost autocratic powers.   At no
period in the history of the Territory or State, not even under
the first territorial governorship, when the Governor had
been given power to appoint all inferior judicial officers,

---

[1] *Laws of the Territory of Wisconsin*, 1836–1838, ,p, 64, Act Dec. 6, 1836.

[2] *Ibid.*, p. 138, Act Dec. 20, 1837.   [3] *L.*, 1839–40, c. 8; c. 41 ; c. 50; c. 85.

[4] *L.*, 1846–48, c. 72.   Indicative of the shifting of local organization and administration are such acts as c. 107 of the laws of 1848–49, which repealed the township organization of Scott county, providing the township boundaries should
thenceforth be merely those of election precincts.

[5] *L.*, 1838–39, Act Jan. 19; *L.*, 1846–47, c. 109.

justices of the peace, sheriffs and clerks of courts, and veto
absolutely the acts of the Legislative Assembly, had a public
officer, within the possible natural limits of his particular
sphere, been given such wide powers.   These powers were
primarily financial, and so administrative.   In the second
place they were judicial.   Thirdly they were, to a degree,
legislative.

His administrative powers were found chiefly in the provision that he should be the " accounting officer and general
agent of the county."   As such he was required to manage
all county business, have the care and custody of all county
property, except such as was by law placed in the custody
of another officer, audit all claims for money against the
county and draw and seal all warrants on the treasurer,
audit and settle accounts of the treasurer and any other
collector or receiver of county revenues and those of any
person entrusted to expend any money of the county.   He
must keep a series of books relating to the various branches
of his office, and, in particular, was required to keep a distinct account with the treasurer.   He must " superintend
the fiscal concerns of the county and secure their management in the best manner."   He was required to keep an
account of the receipts and expenditures of the county, and
make regular statements thereof.   And he was given the
place of a county attorney in civil affairs, being required
to institute and prosecute civil actions brought for the benefit
of the county.[1]   Moreover, the county judge had power
to establish, change and discontinue all county roads and
all public highways not established by the Legislature, to
regulate the care of the poor,[2] to change the boundaries of

[1] *Code*, 1851, § 106.

[2] *Ibid.*, § 129.   These particular powers, with some others, were given to the
" county court" rather than the county judge, but for all practical purposes the
two were the same, and it is needless to distinguish them here.

civil townships,[1] to grant franchises for a long period. And finally, in addition to the above and many miscellaneous duties that they carried with them, some of them widely discretionary, he had the almost inconceivable power to levy taxes and cause them to be collected, though he might not of course exceed the legislative limit.[2] It will be observed how conspicuous—almost unlimited—were his financial powers. Here was local centralization in the administrative machinery of the finances carried to an unusual extreme.

His legislative powers, strictly speaking, were almost entirely those of initiation. He was empowered to submit to the people of the county at elections the question whether money should be borrowed to aid in the erection of public buildings, whether stock should be permitted to run at large, or at what time it should be prohibited, and the question of any other local or police regulation not inconsistent with the laws of the State. And when the warrants of the county were at a depreciated value he might submit the question whether a tax of a higher rate than that provided by law should be levied.[3] While there were thus certain questions that he should submit to the electors, the exact time and conditions of such submission were not prescribed. Moreover, there was a certain indefinite body of local or public questions that he might submit or not, as he pleased. Thus his legislative discretion was wide.

The powers thus conferred were such as, if placed in the hands of corrupt men, could have been used in such a manner "that financial ruin and bankruptcy would have been the inevitable result."[4] They were such that any one

---

[1] *Code*, 1851, § 219.   [2] *Code*, 1851, §§ 454, 485, 1152–1154.   [3] *Code*, 1851, § 106.

[4] For a favorable appreciation of the county judge system, see S. A. Moore, *History of Davis County, Iowa.* The author of this pamphlet had been county judge of this county. Writing in 1876, sixteen years after the system had been abolished, he still favored it.

with the slightest knowledge of democratic antipathy to autocratic power, could prophesy with ease their not remote oversetting.[1] The county judge was to rule for but four years, when a successor might be chosen, but during this period he was little less than a potentate.

Toward the end of the decade, in fact, discontent began to make itself felt. Petitions went up to the Legislature from groups of citizens in many counties, some declaring that the county judge was a tyrant, an autocrat, or the fearful repository of unrighteous authority. Almost none of these petitions mentioned specific cases of corruption or instances of unbridled power, but they were substantially at one in the general principles of their complaint. A petition from Black Hawk county in 1858 put the matter forcibly. It said: " The centralization of such unlimited powers in the hands of a single individual, particularly the power of levying taxes at will, without the expressed or implied consent of the payers—of binding them, as their financial agent, in contracts of which they are ignorant or do not approve—and of arbitrarily expending the public money as his personal interest or caprice may direct—is a policy inconsistent with the fundamental principles of republican government, at all times dangerous and never expedient." [2] Another complained: " With the county funds wholly under his control, coupled with the power to make that fund as large almost as he may wish, there is no balance save the County Judge's own sense of rectitude to regulate the expenditure of the county." The petitions

---

[1] Some limitations were placed upon the power of the judge previous to the abolition of the system. See *L.*, 1852–53, c. 72.

[2] This, with other petitions in the matter, is to be found in Box 40–2235, Vault in the office of the Secretary of State of Iowa. Other counties from which petitions appear are Washington, Jones, Benton, Monona, Bremer, Delaware, Hamilton, Clayton, Jasper, Clinton and Jackson.

called for a divorcement of the administrative power from
the judicial or probate duties, the former to be conferred
upon a board of supervisors or commissioners, the latter
upon the county judge as probate judge only.

At last, after some years of public discussion, the matter
was brought to issue in the State Legislature, and in the
session of 1860 the Senate committee on county and township organization brought in a majority report for a modified supervisor system, and the discontinuance of the county
judge as administrative head. The report was made on
February 13. On February 18 it came up for consideration
and a spirited debate ensued, a minority report proposing
a county judge with two associates chosen from different
parts of the county having been framed to fellow the report
of the majority. The report of the majority attacked the
county judgeship at many points, but primarily and chiefly
on the score of its shortcomings as a financial organ. It
arraigned the system as " inconsistent with the genius of
our institutions, tending, as it does, to centralize rather
than diffuse political power." The report admitted that it
possessed an efficiency above any other, but asserted that
it did not place power where it would always secure the
rights of the people. Of the county judge it said, " secure
in his own councils, he may prepare the way, and in an
unexpected moment strike an unexpected blow that would
paralyze and cripple the energies for years."

It argued that the complex authority of the judge tended
to unfit him for his probate office. For he is chosen " for
his financial ability rather than any attainment that would
entitle him to the position of a Judge of Probate." [1] The
report of the minority evidently proposed only a mild compromise. The writer has been unable to discover a copy,

[1] The Senate Journal does not contain a copy of this report. It may be found
in the columns of the *Iowa City Republican* for February 22, 1860.

but from criticisms in the debates it is evident that the
administrative powers of the judge were to be reduced little
or not at all, and the only check was to be in the creation of
two associates, who should administer the county with him.[1]
In the course of the debate particular cases were pointed
to in which the system had worked unsatisfactorily, a thing
that had been almost wanting in the earlier and more popular complaints. For example, it was asserted that in several counties [2] contracts for costly public buildings had
been made by the judges in defiance of the will of the people,
or that the general interest in other directions had been
thwarted in equally high-handed fashion. Public opinion
was evidently opposed to the system, but it was abolished
not without a contest, and in the public expression upon
the supervisor system which succeeded it there were instances where a return to the county judge was most
vigorously urged.[3]

The administrative and quasi-legislative functions were
transferred to a board of supervisors, consisting of one from
each civil township, except in the case of townships having
a population exceeding 4,000 and less than 8,000, which
were to elect two supervisors, and for each 4,000 inhabitants
over 8,000 one additional.[4] Later this system was substantially modified.[5] The present system is substantially the

[1] See *Iowa City Republican*, February 29, 1860.

[2] Woodbury, Hamilton and Polk. See *Iowa City Republican*, issue as above,
containing a more than usually extended account of this debate.

[3] For example, a petition from Decatur county, containing 422 signatures, filed
some time between 1868 and 1870. The reasons given were that the supervisor
system had cost the county at least 75 per cent. more than the county judge system, that it was far more inconvenient in its practical working, too slow to meet
the wants of paupers, etc. See Box 40–2227, in Vaults of Secretary of State of
Iowa.

[4] *L.*, 1860. c. 46; *Revised Statutes*, 1860, § 303.

[5] *Code*, 1873, §§ 294, 299.

commissioner system.[1] As probate judge the functions of
the county judge continued unabated until 1868, when the
circuit court was established.   In this year each judicial
district was divided into circuits, each of which had its
circuit judge, with original and exclusive jurisdiction in
probate and some other matters, and a wide concurrent
jurisdiction with the district court in civil actions and real
property proceedings.[2] In 1886 the circuit court was in
its turn abolished, the judicial districts reorganized and
the powers of the circuit court, among them the probate,
made over to the district court.[3] Probate powers are now
exercised by judges of the district court, and in large measure by the clerks of such courts.   Thus the last vestige of
the county judgeship as a local organ has disappeared,
and what remained of the office has been merged in the
courts, whose relations bind them more directly to the State
than to any local division.

The system had affected the financial and income administration only for the time being, but during its continuance
it had moulded local financial policy as little else could have
done.   Important as a unique chapter in the financial and
administrative history of the State, it yet had even less
influence upon its subsequent development than did the
State Board of Education upon the development of public
education, and so, but for the possibilities of government
that it suggests, might be considered wholly negligible in
any present discussion.

At this point, from which the income administration may
be traced along several distinct lines, we shall take up the
specific processes through which, since 1850, it has developed
in central or local control, examining the several branches
historically and analytically, to ascertain the degree in which
they have affected the efficiency of government, and the

<hr>

[1] *Code*, 1897, §§ 410, 411.   [2] *L.*, 1868, c. 86.   [3] *L.*, 1886, c. 134.

measure of their influence upon the social welfare of the
people.

III The Processes of Centralization and Decentralization

I THE SEGREGATION OF SOURCES OF INCOME

The study of segregation or the separation of State and
local sources of revenue is of prime importance in the examination of the administrative features of any financial system.   Segregation tends to create and clearly define separate
spheres and organs for State and for local administration.
The State may continue to use the local agencies, and the
locality may continue to use those of the State for a time,
though this is less usual.   But the administrative machinery
for the two spheres tends to separate definitely and com-
pletely when once the sources of the revenue are made distinct, a process that conduces to a great simplification of the
administrative problem.

The place of the peddlers' tax in this connection has been
noted, but it remained for the Code of 1851 and later laws
to blaze the path of separation.   The Code of 1851 provided that foreign insurance companies should be taxed
on their premiums for State and county purposes;[1] after
1868 the tax became one for State purposes solely.[2]   But
corporations generally were to be assessed upon the shares
of stock in the hands of their stockholders.   It was but
natural that insurance companies should receive a somewhat different treatment from other corporations thus early,
as in the revenue laws of the country generally they had
been among the first to receive a distinct treatment.[3]

The law that was to make segregation of material import-

[1] *Code*, 1851, § 464.   [2] *L.*, 1868, c. 138.
[3] *Cf.* E. R. A. Seligman, *Essays in Taxation*, pp. 141, 150.

ance, however, was that of 1862, taxing railroads on their gross earnings.[1] At first they were taxed at the flat rate of one per cent. In 1870 the rate was graduated, running from one per cent. on the first $3,000, or part thereof, per mile to three per cent. on receipts over $6,000 per mile.[2] At first a half was given to the State and a half to the counties. Later the counties fared better, being allowed four-fifths of the proceeds, while the State was to be content with one-fifth.[3] Nothing, under either law, was to be given to the cities. This fact was to wreck the system and bring about a return to the general property tax on railroads. The law had not been a law for long when the cities began to impugn its constitutionality. Several of them had become important points of railroad traffic with large railroad properties situated within their boundaries, a ready revenue for the support of municipal needs, could the law once be converted to their use. The Constitution of 1857 had provided that " The property of all corporations for pecuniary profit shall be subject to taxation the same as that of individuals." [4] Armed with this constitutional defense the city of Davenport, receiving its first favorable decision from the Supreme Court of the State in 1864,[5] pressed its contentions persistently until 1874, when the section was definitely construed and the question of State versus local taxation settled in favor of the cities.[6] The cities were to have a claim to a proportionate share of the revenue from railroads equally with counties or State. By the narrowest margin a constitutional obstacle was thus placed in the way

---

[1] *L.*, 1862, c. 173.   [2] *L.*, 1870, c. 106.   [3] *Idem.*

[4] *Cons.*, art. viii, § 2.

[5] *City of Davenport vs. M. & M. R. R. Co.*, 16 Ia., 348.

[6] *City of Davenport vs. C., R. I. & P. R. R. Co.*, 38 Ia., 633. The important case of *Dunlieth & Dubuque Bridge Co. vs. City of Dubuque*, 32 Ia., 427, decided in 1871, presented the general question squarely.

of segregation. Davenport in its first case had received the favorable decision of the inferior court. On the appeal the supreme bench was evenly divided, so that the finding of the lower court was affirmed only by default of majority. In 1872 railroads were made taxable upon their general property for State and local purposes, the assessment to be made by the Census Board or, as it was now styled, the Executive Council.[1]

But if the constitutional prohibition against difference in the taxation of corporations and individuals was an insuperable obstacle in the way of the segregation of railroad taxes, there seemed to be every reason to suppose that it would be none the less a check to segregation of other corporation taxes, and that localities were entitled to share with the State in their proceeds. Yet the principle of segregation was continued or from time to time adopted with respect to these other corporations. There was no change of principle in the taxation of foreign insurance companies, which since 1868 had been taxable on their premiums for State purposes only. And in 1897 the principle was extended to Iowa companies, which up to that time had been taxable like individuals. Under the Code of 1897 Iowa companies were assessed one per cent. of their premiums, less losses paid, for State purposes.[2] Express companies were made to pay solely State taxes only after several decades, though as early as 1868 they were distinguished for a few years from other corporations, being assessed in each locality where there was an office or agency on forty per cent. of their gross earnings for State, county and municipal purposes. The forty per cent. was listed and returned by the assessor as personal property.[3] Telegraph companies were taxed in the same way. In 1870, as result of litigation, this law was repealed, the taxes under it remaining unpaid

[1] *L.*, 1872, c. 69.   [2] *Code*, 1897, § 1333.   [3] *L.*, 1868, c. 180.

remitted, and the property of telegraph and express companies was to be listed and assessed for taxation in the same manner " as property belonging to individuals." [1]   In 1896, following the recommendation of the Revenue Commission of 1892, express companies were made taxable for State purposes.   They were to pay one per cent. on " the entire receipts from business done " within the State.[2]   Telegraph and telephone companies meanwhile had been made subject to exclusive State taxes.   In 1878 it had been provided that the Executive Council should ascertain the value of the property of telegraph companies,[3] taking into consideration a large variety of items, such as gross earnings, operating expenses, stock, franchises, etc., and on the value so ascertained the council was to determine the rate of the tax, which was to be at the average rate of taxes, State, county, municipal and local, and the taxes so levied were to be in full of all taxes except on real estate and special assessments. This exception does in a minor degree limit the exclusiveness of the State tax.[4]   The Executive Council was required to deduct from the assessment valuation as made by it the actual cash value of the property belonging to the company assessed for taxation in local taxing districts in the State.   So while railroads might not be taxed except for the support of all divisions of the government, these important corporations, the insurance, express, telegraph and telephone, were made tributary to the State treasury, and seemingly there was no one to object.   This was so chiefly because the values were not so large, so obvious, as

[1] *L.*, 1870, c. 100.   [2] *L.*, 1896, c. 2.

[3] *L.*, 1878, c. 59. This law may be said to include telephone companies, for before the taxation of telephone companies was expressly provided for it was held that the provision taxing telegraph companies was applicable to them. See *Iowa Union Telephone Co. vs. Board of Equalization*, 67 Ia., 250.

[4] The same thing, to a greater or less degree, is to be said of substantially all the taxes imposed upon corporations for the " exclusive benefit of the State."

were those of the railroads, and the pecuniary interest was not such as to prompt any one to try very spiritedly the legality of the statute.   When that special interest appeared, when the knowledge of the locality was fully aroused to the fact that a considerable source of revenue was being lost to it, it might be expected that the protest of the cities in the railroad gross receipts State taxes, which, with the Constitution remaining unaltered, the repetitions of statutes could never lay, would be raised anew.

This was done in Polk county in 1899, in the matter of the State taxation of local insurance companies.   There is perhaps no place in the United States where, in a small way, the insurance business thrives as it does in Polk county. The home offices of a large number of life insurance companies of various kinds and of fire insurance companies are to be found in Des Moines, the county seat.   Therefore when in 1897 the State Legislature made local companies subject to a tax on premiums, less losses, for State purposes only and provided that such taxes should be " in full for all taxes, State and local, against such corporations or associations, except taxes on real estate and special assessments," the conditions were made that would provoke a new and earnest contest, for, as stated, such corporations had previously been taxed like ordinary citizens, and from them the localities had derived a revenue.   Polk county gave no heed to the provisions of the new Code of 1897, but in 1899 went forward and assessed the resident insurance companies on the basis of their stock.   Quick to arrest this action, the Hawkeye Insurance Company, an Iowa fire insurance company with head offices in Des Moines, brought an injunction.   Again Article VIII., Section 2, of the Constitution was revamped, and the decisions of the railroad cases reaffirmed.[1]   The county was entitled to tax

[1] *Hawkeye Ins. Co. vs. French, assessor,* 109 Ia., 585.

as well as the State. The opinion of the court was couched
in no uncertain language, and with the exclusive State taxes
on insurance companies there now went down the allied
taxes—those on express, telegraph and telephone companies.

Thus the last and the conclusive blow was dealt to the
segregation of State and local sources so far as corporations are concerned. The spirit of the State Legislatures
had been toward separation of State and local sources, to
a large extent, from 1862 on. And there is ample room for
the opinion that the members of the constitutional convention when framing the section of the Constitution that has
wrought such havoc in the laws, intended no such inhibition
of segregation as has resulted. There is ground here for
a strong argument that judicial interpretation has defeated
the public will and the public interest.

From a condition where segregation might have been
almost perfect, a condition that would in the opinion of
the Revenue Commission of 1892 have meant the entire
divorcement of State and local taxes, the Supreme Court
has brought the revenues to the plane of almost complete
uniformity of revenue for State and locality.

The other steps in segregation need be but briefly noted
here. In 1896 the collateral inheritance tax law was passed,
the proceeds from which go entirely to the State. The tax
on peddlers was transferred to the counties in 1897; though
a new tax, that on itinerant physicians, was reserved to the
State. These taxes and the various miscellaneous income
from State offices, State lands, etc., constitute the only
exclusive State resource at the present time.

An examination of the conditions under which the various
laws were passed will not as a rule reveal any strong agitation for divorcement of State and local income, but rather a
quiet belief that such divorcement would be wise. In the
earlier history of these taxes the inherent difficulty of assess-

ing corporations locally seems more than anything else to have been the cause for their particular treatment. This was largely true with respect to the insurance taxes in 1851 and the railroad gross receipts taxes in 1862. In the case of the latter, however, there grew up a conviction on the part of some prominent in public affairs that complete segregation would be a wise financial policy. In 1872 the Governor commented upon the fact that excepting the State, the counties alone through which the railroads ran received the benefits of taxes from them, and recommended that the tax be made entirely a State tax. His main ground was that the counties receiving the taxes were given a double benefit—the presence of the railroads and a revenue from them—while other portions of the State received nothing. For the sake of equity the change should be made.[1] In that year, however, the general property and general source basis was adopted.

The remaining steps toward separation were made under a more definite conviction of the desirability of the policy. This is shown by the telegraph tax of 1878. Governor Newbold had advised some measures of separation in his message of that year. Furthermore the State express and insurance company taxes of 1896 and 1897 were made exclusive commonwealth taxes in compliance with the recommendation of the Revenue Commission. The inheritance tax, on the other hand, was made a State tax, and not a county tax, as the commission had recommended.

We shall glance now at the material effects of the various steps in segregation. And first of the peddlers' tax or license fee. This tax was from the first little regarded by the local or central administration. We find in the early reports many instances where no attention whatever was given to it. Frequent lapses on the part of

[1] *Gov. Mess.*, 1872, p. 7.

the auditors' reports suddenly followed by a sharp criticism of the local authorities and a statement that the tax would be quadrupled if they performed their duties were characteristic. In the first year the revenue from this source was $222.05 from seven counties.[1] In 1850 it had increased to $836.58, and the Auditor complained that it would be four-fold what it was if those charged with enforcing the law had done so.[2] But there was little attempt to make these local officers collect the tax, and in 1863 the Auditor could report that the peddlers' licenses had added to the revenue only $779.79,[3] and for the whole fourteen years from 1857 to 1871 but $3,787.33 was derived from this source.[4] The receipts improved somewhat in the following years. For the biennial period ending in 1875 they were $1,164.58,[5] but down to 1897, when they were transferred to the counties, they were given very little attention and were insignificant.

When in 1897 the State gave up the peddlers' tax, but undertook to tax itinerant physicians, it was expected that the increase from this tax would not be entirely microscopic. But it has proved so. The license must be obtained from the State Board of Medical Examiners, at a cost of $250 per year. From October 27, 1897, to the middle of 1899 the income of the tax was but $2,750.[6] After that it improved somewhat. From November 14, 1899, to June 19, 1901, it was $3,000.[7] It is to be seen thus that the return from this class of taxes or fees cuts little figure one way or the other.

It is hardly possible to make a computation of the effect of the adoption and abandonment of exclusive State corporation taxes. The chief reason is that such taxes have

---

[1] *Auditor's Report, S. J.*, 1848–49, p. 298.   [2] *Ibid., H. J.*, 1850–51, p. 9.

[3] *Auditor's Report*, 1863, p. 16.   [4] *Ibid.*, 1871, p. 62.   [5] *Ibid.*, 1875, p. 9.

[6] *Treasurer's Report*, 1899, p. 96.   [7] *Ibid.*, 1901, p. 127.

not usually been large, and often they have continued over a period so brief that comparative results would demonstrate little. The gross receipts taxes on railroads from 1862 to 1872 would illustrate little, as they went in large part to the counties. The taxes on telegraph and telephone companies, with the exception of the taxes on insurance companies, afford the instance of longest endurance of a State corporation tax. Beginning in 1878 they continued to 1900, but the income from them was never large. The heaviest receipts from these companies were for the biennial period from 1897 to 1899, when they totaled, from the telegraph companies $40,213.89, and from the telephone companies $18,734.88. Usually the income was in each case $10,000 below these sums. In this same period express companies paid their first exclusive State taxes, a sum of $12,179.71. This, together with the telephone and telegraph taxes, equaled $71,128.48 in a total income to the State of $5,079,403.29. It is apparent at once that little can be predicated upon so slight a proportionate revenue, and that its discontinuance, with the growth in revenue from other specific sources, and the erratic changes to which State budgets are liable, can hardly be reduced to causal relations. Nor in respect of the State insurance taxes can more be said than that they have increased with great regularity, for they still remain. The law of 1900 hardly did more than remove the interdiction of local taxes on domestic companies. It continued the State taxes on non-Iowa companies, and provided that those organized in Iowa should, while subject to local assessment on capital stock, pay the State one per cent. on premiums, less losses, matured endowments, dividends and legal increase in reserve.[1] The State revenue from this source for the period 1881-1883 was

[1] *L.*, 1900, c. 43.

$109,087.43. It increased by steady stages until in 1899-1901 it amounted to $382,165.22.

The receipts from the inheritance tax form more of a basis for estimate. For the period ending June 30, 1899, they amounted to $52,799.52. For that ending June 30, 1901, they amounted to $196,464.54, and formed an important item in the State's revenue.[1]

But this much can be affirmed of the exclusive State taxes in general: they have in the past tended to form an ever increasing proportion of the State's revenue, and this means that the relative part gathered from the counties has tended ever to decrease. In 1899 it was estimated that during the biennial period then just closed but 62 per cent. of the total State revenue was raised by direct taxes on the individual. The remaining 38 per cent. came from fees, taxation of corporations, payments by the counties for the maintenance of their insane, and other miscellaneous sources.[2] And this further fact may be averred of any results here achieved, that whenever the taxes have been separated much has been accomplished to clear up the obscurity of the financial machinery, to make more certain and confident the knowledge of who or what pays the taxes. Such results mean the searching out and the removal of the irregularities of the revenue. The repudiation or destruction of segregation means of course just the opposite.

2 STATE ASSESSMENT

In the history of taxation in Iowa the discussion of State assessment follows naturally upon an examination of the separation of sources of income. For when segregation has failed, recourse has been had immediately to State assessment in several important instances, as though no jot of the

---

[1] *Treasurer's Report*, 1901, p. 9.   [2] *Auditor's Report*, 1899, p. vi.

central control once given were to be sacrificed except under compulsion. This is a most important fact in the development of the income administration.

But State assessment does in fact begin independently of the question of separation of taxes. Its beginning is rather anomalous. In 1858 an act was passed authorizing general banking in the State. Banks and corporations had been under the ban of the Constitution of 1846, and one of the chief reasons for the constitutional convention of 1857 was to bring about the removal of this restriction.[1] This act of 1858 provided for State Bank Commissioners, to be elected by the Legislature. They were authorized to examine the banks of the State, and, among other things, to ascertain the value of the property of the banks for purposes of taxation.[2] This system continued for only a few years, until the abolition of State banking.

The next step in State assessment is to be found in the railroads gross receipts tax of 1862. Under this law the gross receipts were to be reported to the State Treasurer, and the payment of the tax should be to him. While report to and review by the State Treasurer is not assessment as that term is understood in property taxation, still it is as near an approximation to assessment as the peculiar character of a gross receipts tax permits. When in 1872 the gross receipts tax was done away with, and the tax on property valuation substituted, the State assessment was maintained. The law provided that the value of the property should be ascertained by the Executive Council and apportioned among the counties and cities according to their single-track mileage.[3] From the first the Executive Council has been allowed a considerable leeway in the choice of a standard or measure for its assessment, so that centraliza-

---

[1] Shambaugh, *op. cit.*, pp. 219 *et seq.*, 302, 329 *et seq.*   [2] *L.*, 1858, c. 114.
[3] *L.*, 1872, c. 69.

tion in this point is no beggarly thing, but is fraught with
surpassing importance. The law provided that the assessment should be made upon the true cash value, and stated
further that gross receipts should be considered together
with " any and all other matters necessary to enable " the
board to make a just and equitable assessment. This provision has remained practically unaltered until the present.
It has made the method of assessment subject entirely to
the will of the Executive Council, and, especially of late
years, has provoked the keenest controversy as to the proper
basis for railroad taxation. Illustrative of this was the
legislative session of 1902, the interest of which was divided
chiefly between a bill for a more definite basis for the taxation of railroads [1] and one other, which also concerned
railroads. And it is quite generally understood that the
reason why the former bill was defeated was that it threatened the discretionary authority and somewhat secret proceedings of the Executive Council. The bill undertook to
define what should constitute operating expenses, gross
earnings and net earnings, and moreover required that the
Executive Council should publish their votes and proceedings and explain their motives for varying from the market
quotations of securities in assessing the roads. There is
no other branch of the government that at any time awakens
such general and acute interest as does the Executive Council
during the week or two when it is making the railroad
assessment.

In 1875 an agitation began for the State assessment of
telegraph, express, " Pullman " car and fast freight companies.[2] This was strongly advised by the State Auditor

[1] *Senate File*, No. 362, 1902.

[2] For an interesting recommendation that might be interpreted as looking toward
state and local centralization in assessment, see *Gov. Mess.*, 1870, pp. 41, 52.

in that year.[1] The Governors in 1876[2] and in 1878[3] joined in the recommendation, and in 1878 the law was passed providing for State taxation of telegraph companies, the value of the property to be ascertained by the Executive Council. Telephone companies were subsequently included. In 1878, along with telegraph companies, " Pullman " cars were made assessable by the council.[4] The value was not to be taxed to the owners of the cars, but to the companies over whose lines they were operated, which companies were left to their recourse against the owners. Fast freight lines were not subjected to these provisions until 1902.[5] Indeed, there had never been a law for their taxation up to that time.

From 1880 to 1892 questions of equalization and assessment were discussed more than at any other time in the history of the State, but there was no outcome of substantial modification. The chief fruit was the Revenue Commission of 1892. When in 1896 and 1897 gross receipts of express companies and taxes on the premiums of insurance companies, foreign and local, were made payable to the State, the effect was of course to place the ascertainment, or at least the review, of the basis of the computation, and so the quasi-assessment, with the State. But the next great advancement was made in 1900, when express companies, telegraph and telephone companies were made subject to assessment for both State and local purposes on property valuation by the State board of review. This was the second signal instance where, when segregation had failed, State assessment stepped into the breach to preserve the central control. These values are ascertained by the Execu-

---

[1] *Auditor's Report*, 1875, p. 7 ; 1877, p. 8.

[2] *Gov. Mess.*, 1876, p. 4.   [3] *Ibid.*, 1878, p. 6.

[4] *L.*, 1878, c. 114.   [5] *L.*, 1902, c. 62.

tive Council and apportioned to the localities on a mileage
basis.

The advantages of State assessment are obvious.[1]   It is
unembarrassed by the inequalities of local assessment which
constitute so great a drag upon almost all the ordinary property taxes, and, rightly conducted, it provides a machinery
much better fitted than is the local to ascertain with accuracy
the values to be taxed.   In those public service corporations
whose operations are not confined to a locality, State assessment has in the last score of years been recognized throughout a great part of the United States as the indispensable
prerequisite of just and adequate taxation.   Indeed, in the
taxation of railroads while a consensus as to the proper
basis of taxation has hardly been reached, opinion is practically unanimous that when that basis is the general property the assessment must be by the State.   Iowa therefore
in this respect has done no more than keep step with the
progress of the day.

3 STATE EQUALIZATION

From 1850 to the present time the equalization of assessments has been discussed and various measures have been
taken, though none very drastic, to improve it.   But the
problem has always remained a problem.   At no time has it
been believed that a solution was reached.[2]   Improvements
have been wrought; the more crying inequalities of the
taxes have often been leveled.   But disparities have remained, claims of under- and over-assessment have continued, and the remedy that shall cure these ills still remains
for the future.

There are three laws that stand out above all others in

[1] It is interesting to note that the state assessment of railroads was favored and
urged by the railroads themselves, while the cities interested opposed it.

[2] See *Auditor's Report*, 1893, p. 7.

the development of equalization in Iowa. The first is found
in the sections of the Code of 1851, which made the first,
though an abortive, provision for State equalization. This
law provided simply for the equalization of real property
values between counties, the equalization to be made by the
Census Board. In 1853 specific provision was made for
county equalization.[1] In 1857 the second important law
was enacted. It succeeded in putting fresh life into the
anaemic system that the Code of 1851 had created. It p o-
vided only for the equalization of real property values, but
introduced an extension in that it specifically required equalization between towns as well as counties. The third principal law is found in the Code of 1897, by which the State
board was required to equalize not only real property values,
but also personalty. And this law omitted the provision
for equalization between towns.

It is not entirely apparent why the law of 1851, providing
for State equalization, was not put into execution, but that
it was not is measurably certain.[2] For one thing the Census
Board was a new body. Its duties were various, and it
was enough of a strain to bring into play those functions

[1] *L.*, 1852-53, c. 69.

[2] The evidence upon which this statement is based is as follows: (1) The fact
that the record book of the Census Board, which was opened in 1851, on the creation of that body, contains no mention of equalization; (2) the fact that the first
record book of state equalization dates from 1857 ; this book is marked " A," and
search through the vaults of the Auditor of the State failed to reveal anything
anterior to it ; (3) the fact that the reports of the Auditor of State or Treasurer
of State contain no reference to state equalization previous to 1858; (4) the fact
that following the act of 1857, which made more definite provision for state equalization, it was necessary to pass several curative and legalizing statutes to bring
the system into operation, statutes which indicate that state and local equalization
was a new thing, one not well understood and so but slow to become operative.
See *L.*, 1858, c. 90 ; c. 111 ; (5) the comments, or lack of them, upon the revenue system, in the newspapers of the day. See *Dubuque Express and Herald,*
January 16, 1856.

with which in its general character it was perhaps more
intimately concerned than it was with equalization. Moreover, the assessments had not been locally equalized to any
appreciable degree, so that central equalization would have
been a somewhat artificial proceeding.

At this place we should also comment upon a significant
omission from the provisions of the law of 1857, made in
1860. The revenue law of the latter year, while continuing
the provision that the State board should equalize between
towns, did not contain the detailed specifications of the act
of 1857 as to the manner in which this should be done.
This was perhaps an augury of the entire abandonment of
any attempt to distinguish the value of realty in towns from
its value in the county generally, which was to come in the
course of time.

But the chief attempt to reform the equalization laws is
to be found not in any act of the Legislature, but in the
report of the Revenue Commission of 1892. This commission proposed a striking change in the State Board of
Equalization, viz., a partial reorganization by enlargement,
through the addition of eleven persons, one from each congressional district, whose knowledge of values in their several districts would, it was believed, enable the board to
approach more closely to accuracy in the adjustment of the
burdens of taxation. But the device of the commission
went to the base as well as to the head of the structure.
It thought that change was needed on every hand. And so
it recommended important alterations in the county equalization. It would have the equalization in the first instance
made by the assessors and their associates instead of by the
township trustees and town or city councils, who since
1870 [1] had exercised this power. It recommended that the

[1] *L.*, 1870, c. 89. If the suggestion had been followed it would have meant
a reversion to the earlier system of the state.

county board be left as it was, that is, a board made up of
the supervisors, but would require the members of the
local boards to attend its meetings for the purpose of afford-
ing the county board information in the performance of
its duties.[1] Moreover, it recommended that real property
should be assessed only every fifth year instead of every
second year, as it had been, additional assessors to be
appointed to assist in the real property assessment, and,
during the years when such assessment was not made, to
assist in the equalization. These recommendations failed
of enactment, but they are more than a patch-work, and
deserve study in any attempt to better the methods of assessment and equalization.

Study of the workings of the State boards of equalization from the beginning of their activities to the present
time prompts a three-fold criticism, a criticism of the equalization of town realty values, of the equalization of personalty
values, and, in general, of the success, or lack of it, with
which they have adjusted gross values as between counties.

The cases in which the State board of equalization has
equalized the values of urban realty within a county on a
different basis, that is, at a different rate, from the farm
values of the county are, according to the records of the
proceedings of that board, so infrequent that they might
be counted almost upon the fingers of one hand.

At the first meeting of the board, in 1857, there was no
attempt at any equalization either of town or county values.[2]
In 1858 the board, having considered the question of equalizing town property, decided that the amounts reported
from the counties should remain unchanged, the reason
given being that the data were insufficient to justify an

[1] *Report of Revenue Commission*, pp. 12, 13.
[2] *Record of the State Board of Equalization, Book A*, p. 4.

alteration.[1] But as soon as the data were forthcoming the columns of the reports began to show that town lots were included in the general equalization of the county, that is, the per cent. of decrease or increase was made to apply both to town and county values. This is apparent from 1861,[2] and is the almost uninterrupted practice from then till 1897, when, the Code having omitted any provision for the equalization of town values, their amount was left as reported by the counties.

It is evident thus that the equalization was in fact no more than a general county equalization. The law was complied with by including the town values in the flat change and by printing these values as reported and as equalized in columns in part distinct from those containing the county values. Thus a formal but no material difference was established. From this general practice there were several isolated departures. In 1869 the board came to the conclusion that in some instances assessments as between county and city property were very unequal and unjust, city property being valued at a high rate and farm lands at a very low rate. But they expressed themselves as uncertain of their power to change the value of the city or county property without changing both.[3] At the meeting following, however, they had become convinced of their power, and at that meeting, and in 1871, in several cases they increased county values without increasing those of a city within the county,[4] or, leaving

---

[1] *Record of the State Board of Equalization, Book A*, p. 11.

[2] *Ibid.*, p. 28 *et seq.*   [3] *Ibid.*, p. 71.

[4] In 1869, while the values in Lee county were increased 10 per cent., the values in Keokuk, the county seat, were unchanged. *Record of the State Board of Equalization, Book A*, p. 66. In Clinton county, town lots in 1871 were in general exempted from the increase of 25 per cent., to which county values were subjected. *Ibid.*, p. 83.

county values as reported, they decreased those of the city.[1] These exceptions are so infrequent that they are startling when they do occur, and leave one questioning whether they were not the fruit of some abnormal influence. And soon it appears that the board began to recur to its old doubts. Whether its action had been impeached or extraneous influences had bidden it desist is not apparent. But in 1875 we find one of its members, the Auditor of State, declaring, " The State board is unable to make a just equalization, because no authority is given to change the assessment of a city without a corresponding increase or decrease as to all the real estate in the county." [2] And he asked for an amendment to the law. However, it was not made more explicit, and from then on there were no attempts to adjust the values of the town on a basis different from those of the county.

The instances of alterations in personalty values are equally few in number, though this has a more legitimate explanation, the fact that such power was not even to be inferred from the law until 1897. But there is evidence in the early proceedings of the board that they were not fully convinced of their inability to equalize such property, although they did not attempt to exercise the power. Thus in 1858 they expressly resolved that the assessment of the personal property should not be altered, a hint at least of a lingering belief in their power to alter it should they wish.[3] But whatever doubts they may have had upon the matter must have been set at rest in 1876, when the

[1] In 1869, the Pottawattamie county values were not altered, but the values in Council Bluffs were increased 25 per cent. *Ibid.*, p. 66. See also cases of Keokuk and Dubuque in 1871, when, though county values were changed, values in these cities were left as reported. *Ibid.*, p. 82.

[2] *Auditor's Report*, 1875, pp. 5, 6.

[3] *Record of the State Board of Equalization, Book A*, p. 11.

Supreme Court stated, though the statement on this point was *obiter,* that the State board had no power to alter personal property values.[1]

Recommendations of the Revenue Commission and others [2] having in 1897 brought about both the law for the change of real property values by the State board and that providing that it should add to or deduct from "the valuation of each kind or class," the board took the matter up at an early meeting. On July 27, 1898, the board adopted a basis for the equalization of the various classes of live stock.[3] But on July 30, after extended discussion and consideration of the personal property assessment, the board resolved that in the absence of sufficient information any changes would be inexpedient that year. And the Auditor was instructed to prepare schedules of inquiries to be submitted to the county auditors for the purpose of furnishing the board with information in succeeding years sufficient to permit of a just review of the real and personal property assessment.[4] But in no instance do the records contain specific reference to personal property values other than those of live stock.

Finally in 1899 an adjustment of live stock values was undertaken; this was repeated in 1900. But in 1901 there was no change.[5] The values were left as reported from

[1] *Harney vs. Board of Supervisors,* 44 Ia., 203.

[2] In 1885 the State Auditor strongly recommended state equalization of live stock values, but the Governor believed it infeasible. See *Gov. Mess.,* 1886, p. 4. The recommendations of the revenue commission were strongly to this end, but they also urged the equalization of other personalty values.

[3] *Record of the State Board of Equalization, Book B,* p. 152.   [4] *Ibid.,* p. 153.

[5] LIVE STOCK EQUALIZATION.

	Reported actual value.	Adjusted actual value.
1899	$143,988,006	$144,290,970
1900	167,461,261	167,726,884
1901	173,363,731	173,363,731

the counties. Meanwhile no change whatever was made at any time in the values of other personalty. And the failure to adjust such values has been reported quite as a matter of course, without explanation or comment.[1]

The equalization of personal values other than live stock is thus left open, and such values remain, as they have been throughout the entire history of the State, unaltered by any except the local boards. Moreover, the failure to adjust even the live stock values in 1901 seems to threaten if not a discontinuance, at least a broken continuance, of any equalization whatever of personalty. Perhaps it might be urged in defense of the omission in 1901 that the two adjustments preceding had tended to bring the live stock values to something like a correspondence to their true value, but such an explanation is hardly adequate.[2]   A better one would be that the board with its

[1] See matter-of-fact footnotes to tables in *Auditor's Report*, 1899, p. 160; 1901, pp. 155, 196.

[2] Taking several of the more conspicuous cases of alteration in valuation by the board, it is found that:

Values on heifers one year old were increased as follows in 1900:

	Reported average value.	Per cent. increase.	Adjusted average value.
Butler county	$13.58	30	$17.65
Hancock county . . .	12.28	40	17.10
Palo Alto county. . .	12.00	40	16.80

In 1901, when there was no change, these values were reported : Butler Co., $15.80; Hancock Co., $12.02 ; Palo Alto Co., $12.05.

Values on bulls were decreased as follows in 1900 :

	Reported average. value.	Per cent. decrease.	Adjusted average value.
Johnson county . . .	$46.02	20	$36.70
Mills county	47.86	20	38.29
Muscatine county . .	46.25	15	39.32

In 1901, when there was no change, these values were reported : Johnson Co., $44.95 ; Mills Co., $44.16; Muscatine Co., $43.61.

These illustrations might be multiplied indefinitely. They show not only something of the need for equalization in general, but that equalization once begun must be continued. The involuntary change of one year does not insure voluntary justice in the assessment of the next.

present facilities finds it wholly impossible to investigate
adequately values of that elusive and unstable character
that personalty possesses, and so has deemed it best to place
reliance upon those most nearly advised—the local assessors. But to admit that, is to admit weakness in the board
and a need of its reorganization.

From the foregoing discussion it is evident that an estimate of the general results of the equalization of the State
board can be merely an estimate of the adjustment of
general real property values between counties. First cus-
tom, then law, has made impossible the special consideration of city and town realty as such. And the two years
in which live stock values have been equalized throw but
the faintest glimmer of light upon the general question
of the equalization of personalty values. But the numerous
important adjustments made in that brief season indicate
that the need for such action was a very present one. They
indicate, moreover, that the State board when it has a
will to perform its duties can accomplish much.

It is but natural that we should find in the earlier proceedings of the State board greater changes in the per-
centages of decrease and increase than are found in later
years. Property values were less stable, the system of
valuation less accurate in the early years.[1] For the first
years the increase or decrease sometimes was as high as
50 per cent. In 1863 the values of real property were
increased in Allamakee county 50 per cent., while in Buena
Vista county they were decreased 33⅓ per cent. The
values in Boone and Harrison counties were increased 50

[1] For cases illustrative of the instability of values and imperfections of assessment in the earlier period, before state equalization, see *Auditor's Report*, 1848,
S. J., p. 133. There were tremendous variations in some cases. In Scott county,
in 1856, there were assessed 30,000 acres of land less than had been listed in
1855. *Auditor's Report*, 1856, p. 161.

per cent. in 1865; in Franklin county they were decreased 40 per cent. But nowadays even the exceptional changes almost never exceed 25 per cent., while as a rule, if there is any change whatever, it is below 10 per cent.

The sum total of the adjustments in real estate values between counties has been much to the advantage of the State. From 1870 to 1901 the reported values were increased at every equalization, except in 1900, running in amount from a sum under a million to over sixteen millions. This part of their duty the board have performed with a fair degree of success, though it is doubtless true, as the Revenue Commission of 1892 believed, that they have not increased the values of real estate proportionately with the enhancement of their actual values.[1] But if much has been done in the equalization of real values between counties, practically everything remains to be done in their adjustment as between towns, and towns and counties, and in the adjustment of personalty values. One need search no further than the report of the Revenue Commission for proof of this.[2]

4 STATE CONTROL OF LOCAL ADMINISTRATION.

If segregation has not been adopted by a State, or has been provided for or enforced in such a way that certainty has not been secured or responsibility located in the administration of the finances, or if State assessment or State equalization has failed to encompass these ends, there yet exist possible measures whereby they can be realized in greater or less degree. The local administration may be brought to a higher plane of efficiency. This will be attempted in one or both of two ways, either by legislative direction or by administrative supervision and

---

[1] *Report of Revenue Commission*, pp. 13, 14.   [2] *Idem.*

control. The former is the method usually adopted in the United States, notwithstanding its many defects. It is the method that has obtained in most cases in Iowa. So the discussion of central administrative control will be in large measure rather an account of what might have been, but is not.

When the State has drawn to itself the immediate administration of its revenue, of course the local administration is to that extent dispensed with. In Iowa at the present time the central assessment of express, telegraph and telephone companies eliminates their local assessment, and any equalization; the payment of insurance taxes direct to the State treasury eliminates local collection to that extent. And in the past, when at various times telegraph, telephone, express and railroad companies paid taxes only to the State, and transacted the revenue business with State officers solely, local administration of such taxes was in all respects annulled. At the present time, however, there is a wide local administration, and in consequence there abound many opportunities for central direction. The assessment, the primary equalization, the collection and the enforcement of the general property taxes on individuals and on many corporations are in large degree methods of local administration. And in the railroad, the telegraph, telephone and express company taxes the only work of administration not performed by the locality is the assessment and, resultantly, the equalization. Moreover, in the inheritance taxes, because of their peculiar nature, the State has found it economical to make some use of county officers, so that even in this important State tax local administration has a leading place. We shall examine first the administration of the property taxes, and afterwards that of the inheritance tax.

To the question, what is and what has been the State

control of the local administration of the general property tax, outside of the State equalization and the State assessment of the values of the several corporations noted, the answer in general must be that there has been none. The history of the central control in this respect is a negative history. But from the standpoint of recommendations, of legislative effort and plans, it has its positive side. And these will shed some light upon the particular problems of administration here involved.

The most striking fact in the history of this opinion is that the central control of local assessments has never been seriously considered. States have often placed much reliance upon this device, but in Iowa it has been passed by. It has been neglected more than scorned, and it is probable that under favorable conditions and a winning presentment it might attract many adherents. The paramount object of almost every effort to secure a better local administration has been to insure the prompt collection and payment into the treasury of the sums due from the counties on the general State levy. It has been believed by many that the best means to bring this about was to make the counties absolutely responsible for the State levy. This amounted to a proposal for legislative and judicial control. The second, and the only other important means, suggested with any emphasis or at all continuously for the betterment of the relations of State and local organs in matters of finance has been that of a central inspection or direction of local accounts, or the two of these instrumentalities combined. This proposal, like that for the responsibility of the counties, has had in view chiefly the better security of the State income. But with it there has been linked at times a secondary purpose, which now and then has become of almost equal importance with the other. This purpose has been the betterment of county and city finances for the sake of the county and city, and not merely for that of the State. And in this fruitless discussion is to be found the nearest approach that has been made to the central audit of local accounts. To some extent the means taken from time to time to render more dependable the local credits and the local securities, do of course affect the State finance. But as this effect upon it is entirely secondary they will be given but brief attention.

About the earliest phenomenon in the financial history of the State was that of county delinquency. The laggard payment, or the absence of any payment whatever, had from the very outset cost the State a pretty penny. And so from the beginning the State began to consult its interests, asking what improvements could be made in the local administration of the finances. In 1852 the Auditor could report that there were counties that had not settled with the State in from four to eight years preceding, that is, there were cases where they had not even settled with the territorial government, not to say that of the State.[1] The first vigorous step to better the finances was in 1857, when the Governor was authorized to appoint agents to examine the accounts of the school fund commissioners.[2] The looseness of these officers and the consequent losses to the school fund had become notorious, but the reports made upon the investigation were probably a surprise to all but the best informed. Still there was not much improvement in this fund. In 1864 the Legislature attempted to provide for the gradual return of the school money to the State treasury, but the retention of it was left to the discretion of the county supervisor,[3] and succeeding laws did not follow the slender precedent. Before and following this

[1] *Auditor's Report, H. J.*, 1852–53, Appendix, p. 3.
[2] *L.*, 1857, c. 162.   [3] *Gov. Mess.*, 1866, pp. 12, 13.

act there was an agitation for the return of the funds to the State. Governors, financial and school officers advised it on occasion.[1] The State Auditor found the accounts in almost inextricable confusion. The chaos that the school fund commissioners had left to the county judge administration had been affected by the medley of powers of the county judge and his assistants only to make confusion worse confounded. Special investigations were undertaken by local officers from 1864[2] to 1867, and frequently the county clerk had to report to the State Auditor that it would be mere guess work to go back of the reports for the year 1866.[3] In 1862 began the law by which counties were to be made responsible for the school fund.[4] The project of transfer to the State having failed, this was the only means left to secure the fund against loss. But accounts were in disorder; there was the probability that a way of escape would be found from many liabilities by the counties. In 1869, therefore, the State Auditor recommended that he, or some one appointed by him, be authorized to visit the counties and unravel the tangled accounts.[5] This recommendation was repeated in 1871, and in 1872 the responsibility of the counties for the interest on the fund was further enforced, and the Auditor was authorized to employ agents to visit the several counties of the State whose school fund accounts remained unadjusted and under his own direction[6] effect a complete settlement of such accounts. A deputy was designated from the Auditor's office to do the work. Some forty-four counties were visited.

---

[1] *Auditor's Report*, 1867, p. 117. *Contra: Auditor's Report*, 1871, pp. 111, 112. In 1870 the Governor repeated this recommendation, which had been made by his four predecessors. *Gov. Mess.*, 1870, p. 43.

[2] *Auditor's Report*, 1865, p. 47.

[3] *Ibid.*, 1867, p. 76.   [4] *L.*, 1862, c. 148.

[5] *Auditor's Report*, 1869, p. 98.   [6] *L.*, 1872, c. 86.

The aggregate amount gained to the fund by these settlements was reported as $21,837. And the Auditor, in 1873, stated that his report of that year contained the first " full and satisfactory statement of the actual entire available assets of the school fund " in the history of the State.[1] A few years afterwards the official statement was made that the school fund was in prime condition.[2]

This investigation of 1872 seems the only case where there has been a special central examination of local accounts. School funds were subjected to a certain central administrative supervision some years after county responsibility had been provided for. It was provided that where school funds to a certain amount could not be loaned in a particular county the fact could be certified to the Auditor of State, who should order their transfer to some other county or counties where they could be loaned. But it is obvious that this was more by way of assistance to, than control of, the county.[3]

The success of county responsibility for the school funds and its tendency to clarify and simplify the accounts, gave State officers the clue for improvement in the county care of the State levy, and a similar responsibility for the proceeds of such levy was urged. In 1873 the Auditor advised that the counties be held responsible for the full State levy, and that to offset any loss from deductions on account of erroneous assessments they be given all the income from penalties on delinquent taxes, sales of published lands, peddlers' licenses, " and all other additions to the original

---

[1] *Auditor's Report*, 1873, pp. 108, 109.

[2] *Ibid.*, 1877, p. 23. The gradual diminution in the proceeds of the fund has been due to the falling rates of interest rather than to fault in the local custody, though the falling rates have made the loaning increasingly difficult.

[3] *Code*, 1897, § 2856.

amount derived from other sources." [1]   And now, to the middle of the decade 1890-1900, hardly a biennial period passed that both Auditor and Governor did not urge county responsibility in one form or another.[2]   But the Legisture opposed the rising tide of official opinion; no change was made, and the county delinquencies still continue.

Though the means for the improvement of the local administration most favored was that of responsibility, there were throughout many recommendations for central control, or at least central inspection, of local accounts, all of which were equally fruitless.   In 1860 Governor Samuel J. Kirkwood urged that special examiners be appointed in the counties to examine the accounts.[3]   The State Auditor in 1862 recommended that the law prescribe the forms of county accounts or give the Auditor authority to prescribe them.[4]   Recommendations of a like intent followed.[5]   In 1882 a very remarkable bill, entitled "A Bill for a Public Examiner," was introduced in the House of Representatives.[6]   This bill proposed a stringent system for the examination of the accounts of public officers, State and county.   The public examiner was to prescribe and enforce a system of book-keeping and accounts by treasurers of State institutions, and by State and county treasurers, and visit them and inspect their books.   He was to have the same powers to enforce the giving of evidence in the performance of his duties as belong to courts of law, and

---

[1] *Auditor's Report*, pp. 98, 99.   County responsibility was urged much before this, but the agitation did not become persistent till about this time.   See *Gov. Mess.*, 1862, p. 6.

[2] *Auditor's Report*, 1897, p. 6, states that these delinquencies in 1893 were $654,056.84; in 1895, $863,032.86; and in 1897, $971,644.08.

[3] *Gov. Inaugural*, 1860, p. 7;   *Gov. Mess.*, 1862, p. 6.

[4] *Auditor's Report*, 1861, p. 32.   [5] *Gov. Mess.*, 1872, p. 37.

[6] *House File*, 1882, no. 377.

several other important powers were to be given him.
The bill failed, but the Governor in his message of 1884,
referring to this general project, strongly urged the creation
of a body of treasury inspectors.[1] The Governor's recommendation, however, seemingly inspired little comment,
favorable or otherwise.[2]

Little more was said upon the matter until 1899,[3] when
the State Treasurer advised provision for treasury inspectors, who should inspect both the State offices and the
offices of the county treasurers. He called attention to a
number of defalcations and embezzlements which might
not have taken place if the State had been protected in this
way.[4] The Treasurer's recommendation met with the fate
of its predecessors, and central control or audit of local
accounts still remains an unaccomplished desideratum.

Of the local finance as distinct from the State—though
indeed local audit has its inevitable influence upon that of
the State, and local expenditure is to a large extent merely
delegated State expenditure—much may be said that is
favorable.[5] This is due in part to the careful limitation
of the debt-creating and the borrowing and funding powers
of the local divisions and to the comparative rectitude of
the average public servant of the State. The laws whereby
it has been sought to promote economy and sound credit
in the city and town finances have been legion. But all
have provided for legislative, there has been almost no
administrative, control. Administrative control was once
or twice championed by legislator or State officer, but in

[1] *Gov. Mess.*, 1884, p. 39.   [2] *E. g., Iowa State Register*, Jan. 16, 1884.

[3] See. however, *Gov. Mess.*, 1890, p. 33.

[4] *Treasurer's Report*, 1899, pp. xxv, xxvi. Note also his criticism of the lack
of system in respect to various offices of the State, and the lack of unification of
financial methods.

[5] *Cf. Gov. Mess.*, 1890, p. 33.

each case its advocacy proved futile. In 1870 the Governor
constituted himself an inspector of local finance, and, issuing
circulars to the several political corporations of the State,
succeeded in gathering material for a general estimate of
local indebtedness, a thing that had not been done with any
thoroughness before, and that has seldom been attempted
since. During or after these investigations he became
aware that pretended bonds of the unorganized county of
Lyon had been offered for sale repeatedly in New York
city, and he asked that he be given power to bring those
guilty of the fraud to justice.[1] In his next message,
prompted by this instance of fraud, and the many cases in
which bonds, the validity of which had been disputed,
were issued, he submitted to the Legislature the propriety
of enacting a law in which the bonds of cities, towns and
school-districts should be registered by the Auditor of State
upon proof of their legality and security.[2] It is not apparent why he omitted counties.[3] His successor made a
similar recommendation, including counties in his proposal.[4]
But even this slight measure of administrative supervision
met with no favor, and the means employed to improve the
local finances and the local securities were legislative.[1]
Slight qualifications of this statement are to be derived
from such powers as those of the State Auditor to issue
requisitions for information and accounts, or the State
board of review to levy taxes to pay the bonds of counties,
cities, towns or school districts when final judgment has

---

[1] *Gov. Mess.*, 1870, pp. 32, 33.   [2] *Ibid.*, 1871, p. 37.

[3] *Ibid.*, 1874, pp. 45, 46. And see criticism of conditions, in *Auditor's Report*,
1877, p. 20.

[4] In 1876 members of the boards of supervisors in counties having over 4,000
population were made personally responsible for an issue of bonds beyond the
constitutional limit. See *L.*, 1876, c. 125. The Governor in 1878 advised that
the rule be extended to cities, towns and districts. *Gov. Mess.*, p. 32.

been obtained and the proper authorities of such municipal corporations fail to make the levy.

The development of the State inheritance tax law illustrates more forcibly than most things in the history of the finances what administrative improvement can do to advantage the revenue. Several changes in the local administration and additions to the central administrative control have increased the income from this tax in a high degree.

The first two years the returns from the tax were very meagre. From July 4, 1896, to July 1, 1897, only five estates were reported to the treasury department as liable to the tax, and nothing was paid into the treasury in that time. During the second year some additional estates were reported as discovered, but by April 6, 1898, only fifty had been recorded, and the total amount of the tax paid in about two years amounted to but $3,567.08.[1] The cause of this failure was inquired into. It was pointed out that the administrator, executor or trustee, the judge of the district court, the clerk of the court, the Treasurer of State, each at some period in the process of the descent of property, though chiefly the court, was charged with some responsibility. And though the probate or administration and settlement of an estate is not a difficult process, it is often one of many steps and many formalities, so that when complexity in the administration of the tax was added to the inherent complexity in the execution or administration of estates, confusion and the destruction of responsibility might be expected. The Treasurer of State, the officer most concerned in the matter, maintained with much force that the cause of the difficulty was the " lack of responsible, central and systematic control and supervision of the enforcement of the law." [2] He pointed out two means of

---

[1] *Treasurer's Report*, 1899, p. xxxvii.   [2] *Ibid.*, 1897, pp. 44, 45.

improvement, that of giving the Treasurer power to act
directly or that of devolving the collection of the tax upon
the county officials, with a right to a commission on the
amount collected to secure their zealous performance of
the duty. Or, he said, parts of both plans might be employed. He preferred the first.[1] He was also of opinion
that there were grave constitutional objections to the administrative functions that the law required of judicial
officers, and would have them relieved of all such duties.[2]
His criticisms were later confirmed in part by the Attorney-
General and supported by the Governor.[3]

In 1898 a law was passed for the better administration
of the tax.[4] It was provided that the chief justice of the
Supreme Court should appoint five judges of the district
courts to meet with him for the purpose of framing uniform rules and regulations relative to the assessment and
collection of the tax, these rules when made to form a part
of, and be published with, the rules of the district court.
Clerks of the courts were to report lists of heirs and real
estate to the treasury department, as were county attorneys
to the Treasurer. In this way the supervision by the Treasurer was increased. The county attorney was to be allowed
a fee for his services. He was to assist in collecting the
tax under the direction of the Treasurer. Thus the administration was affected both at the center and in the locality.
The fact that the rules for the assessment and collection
of the tax were to be framed by a body of judges, and that
such rules were to have the status of rules of judicial procedure in what was, from the point of view of the State
at least, purely an administrative matter, was a denial of
the recommendations of the Treasurer, who had wished

[1] *Treasurer's Report*, 1897, p. 52.   [2] *Ibid.*, pp. 45, 53.   [3] *Ibid*, 1899, p. xxxvii.
[2] *L.*, 1898, c. 37.

to separate the judicial and administrative services. But
the rules adopted were in a large measure successful. One
in particular, that providing for the appointment of regular
inheritance tax appraisers, met the hearty approval of the
Treasurer.[1] And too much stress is not to be laid upon
the combination of administrative with judicial functions
in this case, for the interests of private law are, in any
question of inheritance, perhaps more crucial than the interests of public law. The interests of heirs, devisees, leg-
atees, executors and administrators are concerned at the
same moment that the public revenue is, and it is not surprising that those officers, the judicial, who everywhere are
made the guardians of private rights should be charged
with a part of the powers of control.

The results of the amendment were immediate and grati-
fying. The revenue from inheritances increased by leaps
and bounds.[2] The Treasurer was alive to this improvement. At the same time he was able to point out instances
in which the income fell far short of what it should be.
He pointed out that if county clerks and attorneys failed
to make the reports, nothing could be done by the State
Treasurer, and the treasury was to this extent at their
mercy. He advised that executors, trustees and administrators be required to certify to the State Treasurer such
parts of their reports as he might demand.[3] This was
provided for the following year,[4] and the Treasurer was
given an important control over the fees to be paid the
county attorneys. In the event of uncertainty or conflict-
ing claims as to the fees due county attorneys he may determine the amount due, to whom payable, and when due,
and so far as possible the determination is to be made in

[1] *Treasurer's Report*, 1899, p. xxxix.　　　[2] *Ante*, p. 187.

[3] *Treasurer's Report*, 1899, pp. liii, liv.　　　[4] *L.*, 1900, c. 51.

accordance with the rules fixed by the Treasurer. But
another and a more vital recommendation was passed over.
The Treasurer here, as in the case of local accounts, asked
for a corps of treasury inspectors who should examine into
the inheritance taxes in the several counties. The suggestion failed of adoption, and there seems no immediate
prospect that the law will provide for these officers.

IV CORRELATION OF THE PROCESSES OF CENTRALIZATION

In the foregoing pages the phenomena of the finances, or,
more particularly, of the State income administration, have
been traced in some detail, and it has been shown that certain broad tendencies are discernible, shaping powerfully
the administration of the public finance. Looked at from
the standpoint of centralization—that point of view from
which the problems of administration can be best understood—it is observed how close is the correlation of these
forces. Judicial decision stands out as the correlating
medium. Judicial decision has grievously arrested the
course of a healthful separation of State and local sources
of revenue, with the attendant prospect of a simplified
administration and a greater certainty in taxation. But
as judicial decision has destroyed, it has also been the occasion of the discovery of forces which to a degree have
served much the same purpose as segregation. These
forces are State assessment, State equalization or State
control of the local administration.

To-day State assessment is the most effective feature of
the central revenue administration in Iowa. Equalization,
though potentially effective, has been of little avail in practice. With a better organization it might accomplish far
more than it has. The State control of the local administration, used as yet only in the inheritance tax, and there,
though not fully, with good effect, has not been given an

adequate test. But it is an expedient rich in promise, and might well employ the zeal of those interested in the financial problem.

The outlook for the future with present laws continued promises no advantage over the past. Indeed, with the destruction of the State taxes on telegraph, telephone and express companies by the courts, and the highly discretionary assessments of the Executive Council to be dealt with, it is probable that revenue controversy will fret the State for many a day. And over all there continue still the great unsolved problems of the general property tax.

But under changed laws and a changed social attitude, a greater stirring of the public interest, improvement could doubtless be made. And these changes would partake in no degree of the odium of reform, for they would be merely old measures or old recommendations made definite, thorough and safe. First of all the State should rid itself of those bonds which restrict the assignment of particular sources of revenue to central or local government. This would require a constitutional amendment, but that is not difficult in a State. To its own freedom and power as a government the State owes this change, and when once accomplished the way will be opened to many betterments. This is not the place for the full advocacy of measures of betterment, but the history of the finance of Iowa must make it appear to the least attentive student that the reorganization of the State board of equalization, the strengthening, modifying and extension of its powers, perhaps the central control of local assessments and the central audit of local accounts—not to speak of a multitude of minor ways of advancement—would make fairer, sounder and more vigorous the finance, and so would improve the social and industrial welfare of the State.

CHAPTER VI

CONCLUSION

THE examination of the laws and documents of the State, of official messages and reports, of public opinion, of the operation and results of administration, bring into prominent relief two cardinal facts in the development of administrative policy and tendency in Iowa. They are these: That while prizing its privileges of local self-government, the local division, be it township, city or county, has never gone to the length, familiar in some of the older States, of making its self-rule a tocsin to be sounded on the slightest threats of encroachment. And the second is that from the very first there has been a willingness to see the State administration exercise authority when it has been made clear that the State was by nature better fitted than the locality to serve the public interest. These are tendencies. They are not rules that will fit every fact in the development of the administration. And they have their exceptions. But exceptions and departures are to be ascribed as much as anything to the obstacles that the structure of government, inevitably patterned after that of the sister States, has imposed. Legislative centralization and administrative decentralization, these are the characteristics of the American State, and in these Iowa has shared. But in the course of time the second of the two, administrative decentralization, has been in a measure corrected. Legislative centralization continues, though administration by the Legislature, of which numerous instances are to be found in the earlier

history of the State, is not so often known at the present
time.

If it were attempted to examine all the branches of the
administration together, with a view to making a general
statement concerning the development of central control,
it would be noted that down to the year 1862 substantially
every branch except public education was decentralized.
In that year the tax on the gross receipts of railways for
State and county purposes opened the way for a degree of
centralization in the income administration. A rather weak
addition is made in 1880, with the creation of the State
Board of Health, but the gradual increase, in other directions, of detail in the State control is sufficient to establish
this year as the beginning of one of the three or four important periods. The creation of the Board of Control in
1898 makes a pronounced addition, and finally the years
1900 and 1902 witness important extension of the State
control of education and health. It is to be observed that
the centralization of charities and corrections, so far as
they were assumed by the State, and of the health administration come comparatively late. But this is largely due
to the later development of these functions of government
as such.

The student of administration will remark the absence of
State administration in the realm of the police, in general
poor relief, in the care of highways and in several more
minor directions. Knowing of the rôle that prohibition of
the manufacture and sale of intoxicating liquors has played
in the history of the State, he will immediately ask if the
State did not itself attempt to secure the enforcement of
these laws by agents under its immediate control. Prohibition has led to the development of State police in some
other States. In Massachusetts, where such a development
took place, the State police were continued even after pro-

hibition was done away with. They were constituted a
sort of State detective corps. But in Iowa the idea of
enforcing the prohibition laws through other than the local
police seems never to have been entertained. This does
not signify that the function of police protection and regulation has been deemed a local function. On the contrary
the local political corporations have not been held responsible for the actions of police officers engaged in the performance of these duties. The courts have expressly said
that they represented the State alone, and that the locality
could not be held liable for breach or wrong by them.[1]

The absence of State administration of the poor relief
would seem to be, in the light of the history of some other
States, in large part attributable to the absence of a State
pauper class. In the coast States, or those where large
cities and large numbers of immigrants are found, frequently the State has to care for the destitute and incapable
who have not gained a local residence. Such conditions
have not existed in Iowa. Moreover, the poor laws have
always been stringent in their provisions that the responsibility shall rest with the county, and that the county if
it fails to transport the pauper beyond the State's limits
shall itself become responsible for his maintenance. And
placing the burden thus upon the county, the State has been
disinclined to go a step further and dictate how that burden
shall be borne. The time is now ripe, however, for some
central control in this matter. The condition of the poor-
houses and poor farms demands direction from without.
The question of poor relief has more than a local meaning.
It has a broad social bearing.

[1] See *Lahner vs. Town of Williams*, 112 Ia., 428, and cases cited. In *Easterly
vs. Town of Irwin*, 99 Ia., 694, it was said : "In the matter of enforcing its police
regulations, the city acts as an agent of the State in the discharge of duties imposed by law for the promotion and preservation of the public good, and not as a
mere private corporation in the management of its corporate concerns."

Nothing has been done in the way of State management of highways. Since the incoming of the railroads, for the supervision of which it may be noted a commission with broad powers was provided, that has been subject to more criticism, favorable and otherwise, than any other in the United States, little or nothing has been done by the State for State roads. Previous to the railroad period a great body of the legislation had to do with State highways and special highway commissions. But the subject of good roads is now one of constant public agitation, and it may be that in due time the attention of the Legislature will be invited to some project for centralization in their management.

State administration has not been known to Iowa in these classes of cases, yet the State has been among the pioneers in some others. The most conspicuous of these is the State Board of Control. But ten States have adopted this high degree of centralization in charities and corrections. And the board created by Minnesota in 1901 was confessedly based upon the Iowa plan. The law by which it was enacted follows with remarkable fidelity that providing for the Iowa board. Another important instance of almost original legislation in central administration was the law providing for the central supervision of milk dealers in the larger cities.

Centralization has led to the entire exclusion of local administration in some cases. In others it has led merely to the central supervision of local authorities. Of the possible methods of central control of local authorities practically all except two are employed. The issuing of rules and orders dealing with affairs locally administered is most conspicuous in the case of the State Board of Health; the decision of appeals, in the case of the State Superintendent of Public Instruction; the administration of local affairs

when local authorities fail to perform their duties or perform them in an unsatisfactory manner, by the State Board
of Health, and by the Board of Control in its relation to
local institutions where the insane are kept; the central
endorsement or accrediting of functions performed locally,
in the work of the State Board of Educational Examiners,
and the High school section of the State Teachers' Association, while the making of reports, diffusion of knowledge, and, to some extent, the holding of inquiries, are to
be found in almost every branch of the administration
examined. But the methods of granting money by the
State upon condition that certain requirements shall be
fulfilled, and the approval of the acts of local authorities
as a prerequisite to their validity, have been employed to
no measurable degree in Iowa. The former method is a
principal one in England, and it has been used with good
results in a number of American States. Under a proper
adjustment of the school support it might be used with
telling effect in the school administration of Iowa, and
possibly in some other branches. And the suggestion is
not an idle one so long as the school fund exists or bills
are introduced for State aid to public schools. The second
of these methods might find its place in the State supervision or audit of local finances, were that advance to be made.

Of course more than a simple ascertainment of the
spheres within which the State and the local control are
to be severally exercised is essential to responsible and efficient administration. There are questions of tenure of
office, of the degree to which under-officials shall be sub-
ordinated to their chiefs, of the bi-partisan or non-partisan
character of the particular board or office, of the relations
of the administration to the Legislature, to the Executive
and to politics. These have been largely considered in
the preceding chapters. Long terms of office have been

established for the members of the Board of Control and for the unpaid Board of Health. In the school administration, however, the administrative head, the State Superintendent, is elected for but two years, though he is usually re-elected. And one would almost say that the administration of the taxes continues to be a political rather than an administrative service, so far as the central control has been organized. To the problem of the appropriate degree of subordination of ministerial officers or those who exercise discretion, within an administrative branch, the Board of Control has given an answer in a large measure successful, while the question of the relation of administration to politics has perhaps been more nearly solved here than elsewhere.

Of the relative merits of unpaid non-professional and salaried professional service the experience of Iowa affords some test. Both systems have been and are employed. The present adjustment is, all things considered, comparatively satisfactory. Unpaid non-professional service failed notoriously in the administration of charities and corrections, and the change to the paid central board worked an immediate advancement. The members thereof because of their judicial or administrative experience may be said to be professionally fitted for their work. In fact in the majority of administrative boards and offices, other than the heads of departments, an informal professional equipment is necessary. Members of the State Board of Health are all professional; members of the State Board of Educational Examiners are largely so; the State Dairy Commissioner, as the statute reads, must have a professional training for his office; and, descending to the lesser offices, some, such as inspectors of mines and oil inspectors, are appointed only upon examination or in accordance with the restrictive regulations of a central board. In the case of the State Board of Health is found an instance of unpaid professional service. But the secretary, who acts as the executive agent of the board, is paid. The boards of trustees of the educational institutions are in their general composition non-professional and unsalaried. They are allowed mileage and a per diem at the present time, though in the earlier history of the state the per diem was wanting. These boards have not been entirely successful; their dependence upon the state legislature and political manipulation have sometimes led to unfortunate results.

The economic causes and justification of central control are almost obvious. The growth of population, the increase of wealth, the elimination of distance through easier communication, have all tended to extend the community of interest beyond the boundaries of the local division and made the state in many ways almost the administrative unit. So late as 1868 it was said that but one-sixth of the lands of the state were enclosed.[1] And in 1870 there were counties having less than a hundred inhabitants that had been organized ten years previously.[2] And as in other states, local communities, even families, were in the earlier period the economic units and almost self-sustaining. But thirty years have changed all this, and now there is no other state in which so large a per cent. of the soil is under cultivation, and few so uniformly settled. And with growth has come a measure of differentiation and the division of labor.

The tendency to centralize is pronounced throughout the United States at the present time. In the year 1901 alone more than forty new state offices or boards were authorized by the various state legislatures, and the principal features of legislation in regard to state government were the increase in these state agencies, the centralizing tendencies in

[1] *Gov. Mess.*, 1868, p. 11.   [2] *Ibid.*, 1870, p. 32.

respect to them, and the increased expenditure for the purpose of state administrative organization.[1] Thus the movement is one of present and future import. Its future extension in Iowa is most probable. Questions will constantly
arise to provoke its consideration. For example, the subject of interurban street railways has within the last year or
two engaged the attention of the legislature, and it can
not be said that the questions of administration involved
have been settled. There are those who believe a measure
of state administrative regulation will be necessary. The
novelty and complexity of the questions involved are such
that there is likely to be a deal of legislative regulation,
which is nothing less than legislative administration. To
any one who examines the charters and ordinances upon
which many of the local railways rest their franchises, which
local companies are chiefly interested in the interurban lines,
it will become clear immediately that the questions which
are to arise will probably fail of a satisfactory settlement if
attempt is made to solve them solely in the General Assembly
without administrative intervention. The case of Des
Moines may be taken as an illustration. Here no less than
a dozen charters and charter modifications now appear in
the city ordinances, at least all nominally affecting the consolidated franchises of the present sole occupant of the city
streets (a company that is extending its lines to the near-by
towns), though it is likely that not more than one or two of
these charters would be relied upon for the company's rights
in the last resort, if the matter were to be brought into litigation. The city hardly knows what its rights are in the
premises, the state is even less informed of its interests.
The question then is an urgent one,—can the public interests
in the interurban railways be conserved through other than

[1] *Review of Legislation,* 1901, New York State Library, *Bulletin* 72, pp. 16, 18.

administrative inquiry and regulation on the part of the
state? For the interurban line is assuredly of more than
local interest. And this is a single illustration of the manner in which the question of state administration arises and
will continue to arise. Many others might be cited, particularly in the branches of administration already established.

The future of state administration in Iowa will depend
upon many things. Constitutional amendment will be
necessary if the taxes are to be made to subserve the highest
public interest. A gradual change, a change already per-
ceptible, in the attitude of the legislature concerning the
proper subjects of legislative control will be necessary. How
often has it been noted in the course of this study that legislative administration is inexpedient, that it tends to violate
the principle of the separation of powers of government,
and approaches the unconstitutional. We can find in the
early history of the state instances where a legislature has
actually gone the length of contracting for the lease of a
penitentiary, and the example is but one of many. The
instances of minute restriction, legalization, formulation of
administrative practice by the legislature can be numbered
by the hundred—all to a greater or less extent perversions of
the legislative function. It is believed that the tendency is
steadily away from this, and therein lies a hope of betterment.

But to the fuller realization of efficiency, responsibility
and independence in administration something more than
constitutional amendment, or changes in legislative method,
or a greater perfection of the details of the administrative
organs themselves will be necessary. There will need to be
a more perfect fashioning of the structure, and a better
understanding of the service of the political party. For the
political party is as much an organ of government as any

branch recognized in a constitution.[1] To some it may
seem that admission of the need of change here puts administrative progress beyond the realm of the possible. But
this is not so. For the very fact that there has been a degree
of centralization has put in operation subtle forces which
will tend to change the position of the party. One part of
a governmental machine cannot be materially altered without affecting every other. There are certain functions of
government that should be secure from political interference.
The judicial function has been universally recognized as
such an one in Anglo-Saxon countries. To this may be
added " the *quasi*-judicial function, the statistical and semi-
scientific functions, and the function of establishing, pre-
serving and developing the governmental organization." [2]
To a degree certain of these functions have been removed
from politics in Iowa. What is the result? To that degree
the function of the party has been reduced to narrow bounds.
Reduction means concentration, intensification. It means
that the play of political forces will become more intelligible
to the popular eye; it means greater publicity of political
activities, hence greater responsibility or responsiveness of
the party to the popular will. In the second place there has
been a measure of transference of administrative control
from locality to state. This has a vital meaning. Under a
decentralized system the elector undertakes to control both
the state and the local government, and ends by controlling
neither. That local choice of state servants is in some cases
wise, is to be admitted, but that that choice when made shall
be with knowledge of the real character of the service to be
rendered, and that the local agent of the state shall be amen-

[1] Frank J. Goodnow, *Politics and Adminstration*, pp. 16, 17, 18; H. J. Ford,
The Rise and Growth of American Politics, p. 220.

[2] Goodnow, *op. cit.*, p. 79.

able to the state's administrative organs—these things are imperative. And it is these things that centralization tends to accomplish. It is impossible here to follow out in detail the full effect of centralization and of the clear definition of spheres of State and local government on politics.[1] But enough has been said to indicate their salutary tendency. Of course these things alone will not make the political party all that it should be,—the sensitive exponent of the will of the state. In America the co-ordination of the expression and the execution of the will of the state is made outside the organization of government, and the means by which the party may be made fully responsible are not easy of ascertainment. Among these means are improvement in election and primary laws, in registration, in the control of parties by the courts; but one of the chief, if not the fundamental means, is that found in the centralization of administration and the nice adjustment that results through it in the relation of township, city, county and commonwealth.

[1] For a full discussion of this important subject see Frank J. Goodnow, *Politics and Administration.*

VITA

THE writer of this dissertation was born in Des Moines, Iowa, January 17, 1876. He was graduated from the West Des Moines High School in 1894. His collegiate training was obtained at the University of Michigan, from which he received the following degrees: In 1899, LL. B.; in 1900, B. L., and in 1901, A. M. He was admitted to the bar of Michigan and to the bar of Iowa in 1899. During the year 1900-1901, which was spent at the University of Michigan in graduate work in finance, administrative law and American history, he compiled *A Twelve-Year Survey of State Railroad Taxation,* the work being *Part V.* of a government publication entitled *Railroads in the United States.* This work was done under the direction of Professor Henry C. Adams, statistician of the Interstate Commerce Commission. He also assisted in economics during that year.

From January to April, 1902, he practiced law at Des Moines. Receiving an appointment in April as University Fellow in Administrative Law in Columbia University, he resumed graduate study, and during the year 1902-1903 he pursued studies at Columbia University in administrative law under Professor F. J. Goodnow, in constitutional law under Professor J. W. Burgess, in political economy and finance under Professor E. R. A. Seligman, and in the history of European law under Professor Munroe Smith.

In addition to the report above noted, he has written *The Iowa Board of Control; a centralized system of administration for State institutions,* published by the Michigan Political Science Association.

225